Visualizing change in small towns and rural areas

P9-ARC-701

ABOVE and BEYOND

Julie Campoli ▪ Elizabeth Humstone ▪ Alex MacLean

APA

Planners Press
American Planning Association
Chicago, Illinois
Washington, D.C.

A B O V E   A N D   B E Y O N D

Copyright to the photographs and illustrations in this book belong to the
authors except where noted. Aerial photographs are by Alex MacLean.
Other photographs are by Julie Campoli and Elizabeth Humstone, except
where noted. Photo manipulations were produced by Julie Campoli and
charts by Elizabeth Humstone.

ISBN (paperback edition): 1-884829-50-3
ISBN (hardbound edition): 1-884829-51-1

Library of Congress Control Number 2001 132025

Printed in the United States of America

To Christopher, Clara, Simon,
Thomas, Eliza, and Avery

CONTENTS

ACKNOWLEDGMENTS

It's been a long journey from a good idea to this book—one we couldn't have made without the many institutions, colleagues, friends, and family members who helped us along the way.

We offer our deepest thanks to our families, John Kassel, Christopher Gignoux, and Kate Conklin, for their combined gifts as critics, advisors, coaches, and supporters.

Mary Cregan went well above and beyond the call of friendship, offering encouragement and helping to make our words clearer and our message stronger. Kathleen Kanz gathered information, checked facts, and read drafts with intelligence, energy, and good humor. Sylvia Lewis of Planners Press urged us with her enthusiasm and determination to make the project work. Sue Kashanski provided skillful editing at the final stages of the book. Carol Hanley lent her considerable talent as a graphic designer. John Brodhead, Gina Campoli, Pam Fox, Ruth Kassel, and Zander Ponzo each offered their insights and perspectives on the drafts. Eleanor Lanahan not only helped to simplify our messages and improve the book's organization but also was reassuring throughout. Claudine Scoville, Libby Hoffman, and Bud and Ruth Kassel provided wonderful writing retreats in Arizona and Maine.

Dolores Hayden, Nancy Levinson, and Jim Shapiro offered encouragement and lent advice. We are grateful to Brian Shupe, Joanna Whitcomb, Melinda Paine-Dupont, David Semperger, Will Fleissig, and Sharon Murray, whose expert suggestions made this a better book. In the air and on the ground Alex's support team included Mike Dupont, Skip Freeman, the Burlington, Vermont, and other air traffic controllers, James Wolff, Eric Greimann, and Mary Sack.

We were able to fly, photograph, travel, and conduct research with funds from the Graham, the LEF, and the Tamarack foundations. We offer our thanks to Randall Arendt, Turner Brooks, Paul Bruhn, Nicky Clarke, Robert Davis, Bill Rawn, Tom Slayton, and Noel Fritzinger for their efforts on our behalf. We are also grateful to the Preservation Trust of Vermont for their sponsorship.

We relied on several institutions to provide material for the book. Ray Godfrey and John St. Onge at the U.S. Department of Agriculture's Natural Resources Conservation Service, Paul Carnahan at the Vermont Historical Society, and Brett Nolte of the University of Vermont Remote Sensing Lab all proved interested in the project and helpful. The staff at the Wilbur Collection and the Map Room of the University of Vermont Library, the Burlington Department of Public Works, the Maine State Planning Office, the Town of Williston, and the City of South Burlington also provided useful information.

Several individuals gathered data, images, or material for us or allowed us to interview them. We offer our thanks to John Austin, Stan Black, Dean Bloch, Doug Blodgett, Pam Boyd, Rex Burke, Marc Companion, Jennifer Ely, Virginia Farley, Larry Fitch, Dan

Higgins, Scott Johnstone, Alan Karnatz, Lee Krohn, Chester Liebs, Kate Lampton, Ginny McGrath, Brian Pine, Jim Pease, Brad Rabinowitz, Connie Snow, Jim Sullivan, Ken Sweetser, Truex, Cullins and Partners, Paul Vachon, Joe Weith, Bob White, and Karen Yacos.

And last, we are indebted to Millard and Helen Humstone, Andrew and Gladys Campoli, and Paul and Alison MacLean for their less obvious but most profound contribution.

Julie Campoli
Elizabeth Humstone
Alex MacLean

October 2001

For most Americans, this is a familiar place (**Fig. I.1**, page x). It's the part of town that wasn't there 40 years ago. This is the place, just outside town, or out near the highway, where we now go to work, buy groceries, and shop. It's also the place we must pass through to get where we're going. Alter the vegetation and the color of the ground, and this could be almost any highway outside any small American city. Car dealerships, fast food restaurants, mini-malls, cineplexes, office buildings, motels, and other businesses are strung out along miles of highway. Each enterprise sits alone on its own pad of asphalt, connected to the road with its own driveway. The buildings, which are low slung, one-story boxes, devoid of detail, leave no lasting impression.

We see this place through the windshield of the car, while idling behind other shoppers and commuters, or while waiting for a left turn. We're anxious to move on. It's not an attractive place. It doesn't inspire community pride or help us feel connected to the natural world. We generally don't like this sprawling mess. We try to avoid it but find that we are bound to it. So we look for greener pastures.

Not long ago, this road *was* the greener pasture (**Fig. I.2,** page xi). It looked like the places we now escape to. In 1937 it was lined with dairy farms and orchards. It offered splendid views to travelers and Sunday drivers, who came just for the pleasure of being here. These two images of past and present show the stark contrast between what was, and what is. But as it happened, the change was not so stark or obvious. It occurred slowly, in very small steps, taken by hundreds of individuals. There was

never a clear understanding of what the result would be, and how each new building or parking lot would affect the whole. In small towns and rural regions across the country, there is a growing interest in protecting the "rural character" of the landscape. This place was rural. Now it is suburban. How did that happen?

This book will try to answer that question. It will examine the development patterns of one corner of America to illustrate a process that is changing the face of rural land across the entire country. Its focus is not on big cities and their suburbs but on smaller towns and regions beyond the metropolitan fringe. This is where change has been slower and its effects more subtle. "Exurbs," "the fringe," or "gateway communities" are some of the names planners have given these places. They are the small cities and villages, the farming towns and byways that haven't yet morphed into suburbs but are now on the verge of change.

Part of the appeal of small town and rural America is that the settlement pattern of an earlier century still dominates the landscape. It's a pattern of compact cities and villages surrounded by large tracts of undeveloped land. Until the middle of the 20th century, before automobile suburbs and before sprawl, this was the prevailing settlement pattern. In this book we refer to it as the traditional pattern. Seeing the differences between this older pattern and a contemporary settlement pattern is what this book is about. If we want to understand how small towns turn into suburbs, how country roads turn into strips, and if we want to prevent this from happening in the future, we must learn to read these patterns.

I.1 Shelburne Road, South Burlington, Vermont, 1995.

I.2 The 1995 photo has been altered to show how the corridor might have looked from the air in the 1930s. A 1937 aerial photo was used as a reference to replicate the older landscape pattern of fields and orchards.

STEPPING BACK

What's the best way to see a pattern? Sometimes by stepping back and looking from a distance. We've stepped way back, into the air, to get some perspective on how the small towns of today are different from those of yesterday. The aerial photographs throughout this book show what can't be perceived from the ground—how it all comes together or, in the case of recent development, how it doesn't. From the air it's easy to see how much space things take up, how individual streets form networks, and what's next to what. The building, the patch of woods, and the town green that we usually see from up close are given new meaning when they're seen in their larger context. This book compares examples of new and old development—highway corridors, downtowns, industrial parks, neighborhoods, farms, and subdivisions—to illustrate two different approaches to using land and building communities. Once we distinguish between the two patterns, we can make a clearer choice about how to shape future development.

The aerial photographs in this book show development in its context and illuminate settlement patterns. We've altered many of those photographs through computer simulation to reveal more: how landscapes are transformed over time and the forces that cause change. Highlighting roads, districts, or buildings shows what is barely seen. Superimposing property lines or land use regulations shows what is not seen. And reconstructing past views shows what used to be but no longer can be seen. These are the techniques applied to images throughout the book to build a comprehensive picture of how landscapes are transformed. Through the manipulation of photographs and maps, we can make the unseen visible, illustrating the development process in a way that makes it more comprehensible.

What are the forces at play that affect the physical form of growth? What can be done to protect and continue a traditional settlement pattern? This book addresses these questions by closely inspecting contemporary and traditional landscapes in Vermont. It uses a graphic approach that *shows* rather than *describes*. It is not intended as a comprehensive catalog of the causes, effects, and solutions to sprawl, but rather as a visual analysis of some of them. Landscapes are shaped by individual choices; local, state and federal policies; corporate decisions; technology; and economic trends. We show images of sample landscapes (the result of a host of decisions) and work backward, explaining how homeowners, businesses, town officials, and consumers had a hand in creating them. In our democratic society, the collective decisions of individuals and local communities have the greatest impact on rural landscapes. But until recently, we've been making these choices without much regard for their collective impact. This book reveals the connection between those decisions and our changing landscape, demonstrating how today's choices will shape tomorrow's landscape.

LAY OF THE LAND

Each chapter addresses a specific trend or issue in contemporary land development. It describes the trend and how it's affecting the form of small towns, and then offers some examples of efforts to counter the trend. Chapter One, "Reading the Patterns," explains how to distinguish between traditional and contemporary development styles. Chapter Two, "Incremental Change," addresses the nature of contemporary development: how we focus on details rather than the big picture, on short-term gains rather than long-term impacts. It shows how small, seemingly insignificant changes add up to major transformations over time. The solution to this myopic approach is town planning: communities taking the initiative to determine the pattern of growth in their town. This means remembering the past, imagining the future, and setting up a framework within which a desirable pattern can emerge.

Chapter Three, "Edges and Centers," illustrates the movement of population, commerce, and investment from the centers to the edges of older cities and villages. This trend, which has been occurring in metropolitan regions for almost a century, has more recently affected the small cities and towns in rural areas. We review the impact of this outward migration, showing how personal choices and public policies create a growth pattern that bloats the edge and drains the center. Although contemporary development overwhelmingly favors growth on the edge, this chapter demonstrates some ways towns that can draw clearer boundaries and reinvigorate the center.

Spreading out and its effects on the working landscape and wilderness of rural areas is the topic of Chapter Four, "Fragmentation." Here we examine the costs to farms, to outdoor recreation, and to wildlife of low-density, scattered development. It illustrates how country homes and remotely located businesses are, bit by bit, nibbling away at fields and forests. We look at the causes: our urge to live in the country, our faulty planning processes, our tendency to squander space. And we show examples of how we can alter this pattern through better regulations, land conservation, and luring homebuyers back to the village.

Our tendency to allocate separate areas of town for living, working, shopping, and playing is the topic of Chapter Five, "Separation." This chapter explains why everywhere you need to go is so far from wherever you happen to be. The traditional pattern of layering and integrating a rich mix of housing, offices, parks, and factories into a small area is contrasted with this more contemporary one. In addition, examples are offered of homogeneous residential areas with little or no income or ethnic diversity. We show how zoning, public policy, and public investments encourage us to segregate the functions of everyday life into horizontal, compartmentalized suburbs, forcing us to spend more time in the car. Weary of traffic and isolation, people across the country are seeking ways to integrate working, living, shopping, and recreation. This requires community support for mixed uses and housing types as well as governmental action that fosters diversity.

In Chapter Six, "Private Space, Public Realm," we show how Americans' recent obsession with privacy and control has influenced the way they arrange their workplaces and homes. We illustrate the neglect of public spaces and the dominance of private interests in contemporary development, comparing these trends to an earlier era when public space was valued and community life was accommodated in the layout of towns. "Private Space, Public Realm" shows how the fabric of older towns nurtures a sense of identity and community, and how this traditional pattern can be replicated in contemporary development.

One of the biggest differences between traditional and contemporary settlement patterns is the size of old versus new development. The trend toward bigger houses, stores, warehouses, offices, and roads is covered in Chapter Seven, "Scale." We look at our increasing appetite for space and how we accommodate our desires through the consumption of larger and larger parcels of land. The costs are high, as municipalities struggle to maintain far-flung roads and sewer, water, and utility lines. Communities can help slow this trend by setting limits on the size of retail buildings, improving the quality of city and village neighborhoods, and rewriting their land use regulations to allow for compact development.

"Cars" illustrates how the automobile sets the pattern of contemporary development. We examine two aspects of the car that wreak havoc on the landscape: its size and its speed. Cars are an essential part of life in small towns, and where the population is low, their impact is limited. But as small towns grow, they face the prospect of slipping into suburbs if their attitude toward the car doesn't shift along with their population. This chapter describes a more urban approach to cars in which a thrifty use of space and a reliance on walking replaces the "cars rule" mentality of suburban development.

Throughout this book, we examine the different sides of ourselves that are often at odds: the side that wants to belong to a tightly knit community and the side that wants to live apart, the side that seeks a balanced relationship with nature and the more consumer-oriented part of us that ignores the limits of natural resources. The community planning efforts described here are a way to balance these conflicting impulses. The examples of planning commissions, nonprofit organizations, and state and local governments developing plans, revamping regulations, and protecting open land show how individuals acting collectively can create an alternative to sprawl.

1.1 Vergennes, Vermont.

The following section provides a sample of some of the land settlement patterns that are featured in the book. Unlike the succeeding chapters, the emphasis here is on recognizing the form of traditional versus contemporary patterns, rather than the causes or effects of those patterns. Aerial photographs of towns that predate World War II are paired with images of recent growth. The accompanying text points out the differences.

Figures 1.1 and 1.2 show contrasting patterns of street and land use. At the top is an older town, Vergennes, Vermont, and at the bottom, a new growth area, Mashpee, Massachusetts. In the traditional pattern, several regional roads converge at a village where the building pattern is denser than it is in the areas surrounding it. The streets are hard to see from this elevation because they're not wide and many are lined with trees, but they form an interconnected grid system that creates small blocks in the village and provides links between through roads.

Growth in Mashpee is also located at the convergence of roads, but unlike Vergennes, Mashpee has no central area where buildings are concentrated. They are dispersed across a broader area. In Vergennes, a secondary system of back streets provides frontage for development. This is not the case in Mashpee, where all the buildings are reached from the arterial roads, which are fewer in number but wide. Buildings don't line the street, as they do above, but sit apart, each with its own self-contained road network.

1.2 Mashpee, Massachusetts.

1.3 Fair Haven, Vermont.

1.4 Essex, Vermont.

The centralized pattern in Vergennes leaves large blocks of land undeveloped while the pattern of built and open space in Mashpee is fragmented. In Vergennes, the village as a whole is surrounded by open space. But in Mashpee, each development is ringed with a small patch of woods.

The green space in the center of Fair Haven, Vermont, is shared by all the buildings around it (**Fig. 1.3**). Trees and lawn are not used to separate structures and activities but to bring them together. In this traditional pattern, buildings have small footprints. They don't take up much space on the ground, but they provide floor space vertically, by extending upward to five stories. There is a mix of single-family homes, apartments, businesses, and institutions within a small area. The compact arrangement makes walking the quickest and easiest way to travel between buildings.

In Essex, Vermont (**Fig. 1.4**), driving is the best way to get from one place to the next. Buildings take up more ground space and are far apart. With the exception of the houses in the foreground, all the buildings shown are one story high. They use horizontal rather than vertical space, so they must stretch across a wider area. Unlike Fair Haven's, Essex's land is divided horizontally according to function. Homes are in the foreground, retail is in the background, with substantial distance separating the two. As in Mashpee, these developments have circulation systems that are unconnected with nearby buildings.

In Fair Haven, the buildings hug the street, forming a wall that defines the main shopping street. Take away the pavement and the path of the street would still be clear. This is not the case in Essex, where the pattern

1.5 *Newbury, Vermont.*

1.6 *South Burlington, Vermont, and Shelburne, Vermont.*

of buildings is not related to a street. Imagine the asphalt gone from the shopping center: Can you guess where the road goes?

Figures 1.5 and 1.6 show two different patterns of linear development. Both consist of buildings laid out along a road corridor, but one is a village center and the other is a commercial strip highway. How can a similar arrangement create two such different environments? The biggest discrepancy between the two patterns is in scale. In Newbury, Vermont, parcels are narrow and front yards are small. Buildings hug the street and sit close together. The result is a pattern of small-scale buildings lining the street: the basic structure of a village street. The narrow setback leaves land open at the rear of each lot, where much of the space is used for agriculture.

In South Burlington, Vermont, linear development is at a scale that fits the size of automobiles. Lots and buildings are larger than in Newbury, and the green space is not in the rear but in the front of the buildings. Here it takes the form of a "buffer" rather than a field, and it is not contiguous with other open areas.

As in Mashpee, properties are reached only by travel on the main highway, with no direct connections between them. Each has its own circulation system and is surrounded with its own parking area. Typical of commercial strip highways, there are no large trees lining the road. Visibility for passing motorists is given priority, and trees are considered an obstruction.

In the traditional pattern, shown on page 4 (**Fig. 1.7**), there is a hierarchy of spaces—a central area that is the focus of the community surrounded by peripheral districts and neighborhoods. This is a view of Burlington,

1.7 Burlington, Vermont.

Vermont, showing a difference between the downtown center and the residential areas that flank it. There is a clear distinction between the tight arrangement of higher, bigger buildings in the center and the less dense, greener areas that make up the city's neighborhoods.

In a contemporary pattern, such as that seen in Colchester, Vermont (**Fig. 1.8**), there is no central focus for development and no hierarchy of districts emanating from a central point. Development is divided evenly among four quadrants of an interstate highway interchange. The uses are similar in each section, and so are the siting and form of the structures.

In this area of Colchester, the street system consists of one artery (running top to bottom in the photo) and many private driveways. The interstate cuts the area in two, preventing street connections between neighboring businesses. Anyone travelling from one building to another could follow only one route. There are no short cuts. Contrast this with Burlington, where a grid of many streets ties each building to the whole network. There are many paths to the same destination. As a result, the traffic is dispersed over many narrow streets. In Colchester, one artery must carry it all. As traffic grows, so does the width of the road.

Figures 1.9 and 1.10 show two different neighborhood patterns. Figure 1.9 was taken in an older section of Waterbury, Vermont, Fig. 1.10 in a new subdivision of Essex Junction. Perhaps the biggest difference between the two patterns is in the orientation of the buildings and how they are placed on their lots. In Waterbury, the houses are set very close to the street with their long sides perpendicular to it. The lots are narrow, and these houses

1.8 Winooski, Vermont, and Colchester, Vermont.

1.9 Waterbury, Vermont.

1.10 Essex Junction, Vermont.

were sited to make the best of it. Front yards are short, but rear yards are deep.

In Essex Junction, the lots are shallow and wide. Houses are aligned with their long sides parallel to the street, and each home sits in the middle of its lot. Front, rear, and side yards are roughly the same size. The distance between front doors in Waterbury is about 50 feet. In Essex it's roughly 90 feet.

In the traditional pattern, garages don't sit along the front plane of the building but are set back, behind the house. The driveway runs along the side of the house creating a service courtyard that is less visible from the street. In Essex Junction, garages are large and driveways wide. They are not tucked behind or behind the house but out in front.

The siting of commercial buildings in Ayer, Massachusetts (**Fig. 1.11**, page 6), follows the traditional pattern typical of many small villages. There are seven structures here, but because they butt up against each other, they function as a block. Their facades form a continuous line along the sidewalk that directly connects each store entrance. Cars are parked along the street or in a shared lot behind the buildings. Walkways and alleys link the rear parking lot to the sidewalk in front.

This older pattern contrasts sharply with the more contemporary strip development pattern seen in Bennington, Vermont (**Fig. 1.12**, page 6). These buildings are isolated by an auto-oriented circulation system. The parking and service areas that surround each structure push it away from its neighbor and away from the street. There is no shared space here. As in

1.11 Ayer, Massachusetts

1.12 Bennington, Vermont.

Ayer, a sidewalk runs the length of the block, but it does not hug the buildings. Parking lots and driveways stand between the sidewalk and store entrances.

Here are two different ways to site buildings in the countryside. **Figure 1.13** was taken in Waitsfield, Vermont; it illustrates a traditional pattern. The photo of a hillside in Stowe, Vermont (**Fig. 1.14**), shows how homes are often sited today. In the traditional pattern, land is used to produce food. Space in the larger buildings is used to shelter livestock or to store feed and machinery. In the contemporary pattern, buildings are also large, but they provide personal living space. Here, land is used for leisure.

The buildings in Waitsfield are located in a populated valley along a through road. Those in Stowe are set on a remote, forested hillside. The buildings at left hug the road, occupying the edge between the highway and the fields. The ones at right are set apart, in the center of a clearing. The farm structures are aligned with the geometry of the road, while the Stowe homes are oriented to the view of surrounding hills.

1.13 Waitsfield, Vermont.

1.14 Stowe, Vermont.

2.2 A 1999 close-up view of Shelburne Road as it runs through South Burlington, Vermont.

2.3 A simulated view of the landscape pattern along Shelburne Road in the 1930s.

2.4 An actual view of Shelburne Road taken in 1995.

SMALL STEPS, BIG CHANGES

The very first photographs in this book show a before and after view of a highway corridor running through South Burlington, Vermont. Until recently, this area, known locally as Shelburne Road, was an unbroken stretch of farm fields and orchards. Now it's a commercial strip highway. The images show two points on a development continuum. It was one thing, now it's another. But what about all the stages in between? How did it change from farm fields into a suburban strip?

It was transformed in small, seemingly insignificant steps (**Figs. 2.2-2.4**). This is the nature of growth in small towns and rural areas. Unlike metropolitan regions, where 200-unit subdivisions and "big box" stores seem to appear overnight, the pace and scale of growth in rural America typically comes in smaller increments. Because change happens slowly, it's easy to imagine that it won't happen at all. Growth is usually unanticipated, and, for a long time, barely perceptible. If change seems implausible, then planning for it seems unnecessary and unlikely.

This chapter illustrates how, without a deliberate effort to plan for an alternative, small towns are destined to grow in a sprawling pattern. It shows how the decisions made by many people randomly accumulate into an outcome that is welcomed by few. The pattern of growth—what gets put where and what form it takes—is set by an underlying framework. Today, that framework produces sprawl, but not long ago, a different development framework produced a traditional pattern. Communities that choose to grow in a traditional, compact pattern can alter the framework so that all the small steps lead to a change they want.

As rural areas grow, there is often no clear turning point, only a slow evolution. In the transition from a pastoral to a suburban landscape, each increment of change subtly alters the ratio of developed to open land. Add a subdivision, subtract an orchard. Add a restaurant, subtract a pasture. In the early stages, there is so much open land that additions are barely noticeable. The odd restaurant or gas station on a country road doesn't seem obtrusive when it is set before a backdrop of green hills. But as more land is altered and the ratio shifts, the character of the road changes.

The transformation of Shelburne Road took place continuously, but the process can be better understood when it is examined in stages. **Figures 2.5 through 2.8** show what the road looked like at various points in time. In 1937 two different patterns were visible. The grid of streets with houses close together on small lots marked the edge of the city. To the south, clusters of farm buildings appeared at regular intervals along the highway. Although there were several buildings along the road, many of these structures were barns. The land was used for farming and was sparsely populated. In 1937, with large open tracts of land, there was a sharp distinction between the inside and the outside of the city.

The 1962 map shows a transition between rural and suburban settlement patterns. A few large farm parcels were subdivided in the 1950s and are shown on this map as new neighborhoods. These were followed by two shopping centers. Between 1937 and 1962, tourist services flourished along the road. Restaurants, motels, and antique shops appeared, locating close to the traveled way to attract passing motorists. Many of the farm buildings and open fields remained, as farm operations coexisted with the newer businesses.

By 1974, the new growth was geared less to the tourist market and more to the new residents of South Burlington. Many of the businesses that appeared during this period had relocated from the neighboring city of Burlington. On the highway, they could expand and provide free parking to their customers. The new buildings were bigger than the existing farm and motel structures and included more spacious parking areas. A spur to the nearby interstate had been completed in the mid-1960s, and shortly after, another shopping center appeared. Several downtown car dealers had closed their showrooms downtown and set up shop on the strip. By 1974, the older, rural pattern had been eclipsed. [1]

By 1996, it had virtually gone. Commercial development had filled in along a wider band. At the outer fringes of the corridor, a few new residential streets had been built with several condominium complexes cropping up beside the new shopping centers. Currently, there are three tiers of development along the highway. Retail stores, restaurants, and the remaining motels occupy the land closest to the road. More recent industrial and office buildings as well as apartments and condominiums sit in the middle tier. On the outer fringes of the strip lie single-family homes. A few remnants of open land appear on this 1996 map, but they have since been claimed by a supermarket and an office expansion. It took 60 years of lot-by-lot additions, but eventually, the whole corridor was transformed.

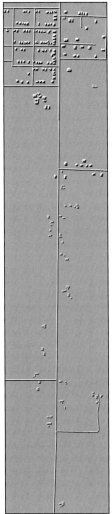

2.5 1937

2.5 thru 2.8 Four snapshots of the
changing pattern on Shelburne Road,
South Burlington, Vermont.

2.6 1962

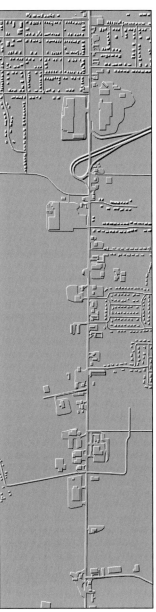

2.7 1974

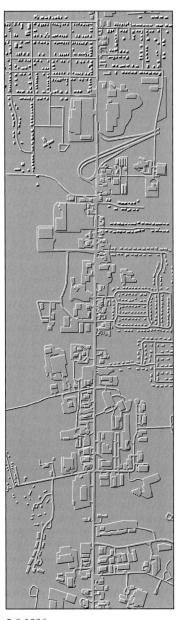

2.8 1996

2.9 *An undeveloped intersection with land for sale.*

2.10 *The rural context remains strong although a business has located here.*

2.11 *A higher ratio of buildings and parking to open land makes the highway look more like a strip and less like a rural road.*

2.12 *A road eventually becomes a commercial strip as the gaps are filled with parking areas.*

Without much growth pressure, changes occur slowly. And because smaller scale change is not visually prominent, it's easy for most residents of a town to assume that rural land will remain rural forever.

Four photographs illustrate the gradual nibbling away of open land that is typical along rural highways. Taken in four different locations, they represent various stages in the process of strip development.

The first view (**Fig. 2.9**) shows land at an entirely undeveloped intersection outside a small village. Only the "for sale" sign indicates that a change may occur here. The owner of the land is hoping that someone will see the commercial potential of this parcel and offer a good price. But for now, it's just a possibility.

In the second photograph (**Fig. 2.10**), someone has established a business on the edge of this highway. It's small and unassuming. Although there is a large parking lot with several cars parked in front, the absence of any other buildings in the area and the view of fields and woods beyond give the impression that this is still "the country."

With the addition of a few more businesses, the scene would look similar to **Fig. 2.11**. This place is more settled than the previous two and has a very different character. There is a higher ratio of paved and built area to open land, which gives it a more suburban appearance. This place has begun to look less like a country road and more like a strip highway.

The transition is even more complete in **Fig. 2.12**. On the left side of the road, there are no gaps left between developed parcels. The visual impact of parked cars is more pronounced than in the photo above it because there are more parking lots and more vehicles in relation to the surrounding land. Not long ago, this place looked like **Fig. 2.9**. It changed slowly, and at other points of time, resembled the two other places shown here. Most likely, it will continue to grow in the same pattern, with the natural context receding further into the background, ultimately evolving into a commercial strip highway.

These images represent what is happening to the ordinary landscape of rural areas. These places may not be visually remarkable but they are widely seen. Because we travel these corridors on a regular basis, the view has a big effect on our experience of a place. But when the steps are small and the scenery unremarkable, it is hard to become alarmed. The little additions and alterations along roadways over time add up to a substantial change, but the change usually goes unnoticed until it's too late.

Change is even less obvious in other rural areas where densities are low and human impact on the land seems minimal. A few new houses on a wooded hillside and one more in the nearby meadow don't transform the countryside. But again, as incremental changes add up, the impact grows.

The landscape of Norwich, Vermont, shows this cumulative change. Bit by bit between 1963 and 1996, a newer settlement pattern was overlaid on the traditional pattern of open fields and forested hillsides.[2]

The earlier pattern (**Fig. 2.13**) was shaped by the needs of agriculture and the limitations of the technology and the economy of the era. To limit road costs and save arable land, buildings were located close to the public byways. Because most of the buildings were farm related, they were sited not on steep, wooded hillsides but adjacent to the richer, more level soils.

Thirty-five years later, those buildings are still there, but they have been joined by many other structures that were sited with an entirely different logic (**Fig. 2.14**). For the individuals who built houses after 1963, road costs and transportation were no longer limiting factors. Not being farmers, they felt no pressing need to preserve tillable fields, only privacy and views. As a result, many of the newer buildings are isolated in the woods, at the tops of hills or on open meadows. Earlier buildings clung to the through roads; later ones were located far from them. Dead-end streets and long driveways were grafted onto the original road network, pushing houses farther away from passing cars.

Since 1963, this landscape has been developed without a clear understanding of what its long-term future would be. As each individual builds to take advantage of the pastoral view, that resource is diminished. Agriculture fades as the land is carved up, and newer houses intrude on the neighbor's view (**Fig. 2.15**). In the earlier period the pattern was based on protecting the resource, namely productive land. In the recent one, the resource is a natural setting and the pattern is gradually consuming it.

The use of land and the level of human activity on it play a role in how we perceive its character. For example, a lake with a wild, undeveloped shoreline is quite different from one dotted with summer camps. But that seems primitive compared to one ringed with year-round homes. As human use along a shoreline incrementally increases, there is time to adjust to the growing impact on the land. The same acclimatization happens as we adapt to slow development along a rural highway or in an outlying farm district like the one in South Burlington. Each step in the process brings a more intense use, which makes the next step more palatable. And while commercial strip development and scattered residential housing might not have been what these communities wanted, it's what all the small steps eventually led to.

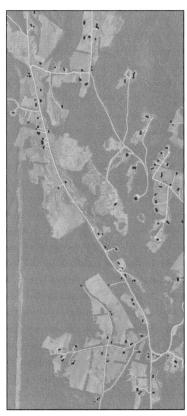

2.15 Norwich, Vermont, 1995. The contemporary pattern, with houses set back from the road on higher ground, is apparent here.

2.13 Norwich, Vermont, 1963. Buildings (in red) were located close to the public byways. Because most of the buildings were used for farming, they were sited not on steep, wooded hills but on level land close to richer soil.

2.14 Norwich, Vermont, 1996. Newer buildings are constructed in the woods, at the tops of hills, or on open meadows, at the end of long driveways.

2.16 About 20 years ago, this area was sparsely populated and served as a transition between the more developed valley below (not shown) and the wilderness area of the Green Mountain National Forest (simulated image).

2.17 A regional bypass introduced high traffic volumes to the area. An interchange and connector road offered excellent access to a major road, dramatically increasing this area's development potential (simulated image).

2.18 Low-density development filled up the newly designated commercial zone. The western side of the corridor had become a suburban outpost (simulated image).

2.19 The outpost spread to the other side of the corridor when a company got permission to upgrade the interchange (actual photograph).

Figures 2.16 through 2.19 illustrate how a series of steps can change perceptions about land and affect our decisions about how to use it. They also show how land use choices can have unintended effects. **Figure 2.19** is an actual photograph. The other three images have been altered to show different points in time. Together, they show several steps in the sequence that transformed a remote section of Sunderland, Vermont, into a commercial area.

The first image (**Fig. 2.16**), depicts what the land looked like about 20 years ago. A back road served a few farm fields and a handful of houses that sat at the edge of a high elevation upland forest that runs for miles along the western flank of the Green Mountains.[3] This area was the sparsely populated transition between the more developed valley below it and the wilderness area of the Green Mountain National Forest. Except for the residents of the dead-end road and the occasional hunter or hiker, few people ever saw this land.

In the 1960s congestion along the historic highway lower in the valley (U.S. Route 7) had become a frustration. Seeking an alternative route, transportation planners saw this higher corridor as a suitable location for a new regional bypass. They believed a new, faster road would get trucks out of the villages and speed long-distance travel. As planned, this new highway would be "limited access," meaning that its controlled entrance and exit points would prevent the type of strip development that had clogged the older road. This would be a through highway, not a developed corridor. Growth would remain lower down the valley, along Route

7, near the villages and settled areas.[4] The second image (**Fig. 2.17**), shows the new highway and the road connecting it to Route 7, 1.5 miles away. At this point in time, there were no new developments, but the land had become visible and accessible. Although no one stopped, thousands passed through every day.

No developments were allowed direct access onto the new highway, but the state transportation agency could not control *indirect* access to it. The newly constructed connector road (perpendicular to the highway) provided an easy link between the land surrounding the interchange and the highway. The new road had created a sweet spot for auto-oriented development: open land beside an interchange. It seemed like a windfall for the tiny rural town of Sunderland, which zoned the interchange for commercial/industrial use. In the following years, businesses moved to this area to be nearer to the new highway. The old farm fields provided a handy spot to site buildings and parking lots (**Fig. 2.18**). The presence of an existing settlement, however sparse, made it easier to envision the land as developable. It was no longer remote. It was just another small step to intensify its use. Within a few years, the western side of the corridor became a small outpost of commercial development.

In the late 1990s the outpost jumped to the other side of the highway when a local company, an outdoor outfitter, moved its headquarters from a nearby town center to the hill above the road (**Fig. 2.19**). The intersection had been designed to restrict entrance to this site, but the business had no trouble securing a permit from the state transportation board to upgrade

KEY: upgraded state highway   water lines   property lines

commercial zone   sewer lines   setback area

2.20 The unseen framework made visible. This image reveals the unseen infrastructure and land use regulations that shaped development along Shelburne Road in South Burlington, Vermont. Sewer and water lines, highway improvements, zoning districts, property lines and site design regulations have been drawn onto Fig. I.1. The zoning lines show the large amount of land dedicated to one use.

the interchange. The site was irresistible. It had great views, was right beside the highway, and provided plenty of space. And being in the woods, it seemed to fit the company's outdoor image. Another small step was taken, this time, into the forest.

But all the little steps—the bypass, the access road, the commercial zone, the office complex—added up to a giant leap up the hill. And it was heading straight into the heart of a wilderness and recreation area. When the company sought a permit from the environmental review board, the impact became clearer. This was prime bear habitat and part of a regional migration corridor. As part of its permit condition, the company was required to grant conservation easements around its property, essentially sealing off the rest of the land from access to the highway. The nibbling away of the forest was stopped at this particular location.

The series of decisions that transformed this landscape were made for different reasons: to solve a transportation problem, to encourage economic development, to create an idyllic corporate campus. Each was a response to existing conditions, and each had unintended consequences. What was missing was an overall view of the bigger direction—where all the small choices were leading.

THE HIDDEN FRAMEWORK

Landscapes are shaped by a series of many individual decisions. But these choices are not arbitrary. For the most part, they are based on a set of factors—an underlying land development structure. This is the hidden framework that shapes growth in every town. It consists of a mix of physical factors and cultural, technological, political, and economic forces that manifests itself in public policies, public investment decisions, and market forces.

Some of the elements of this unseen framework can be made visible. In **Figure 2.20**, the framework for development is superimposed on Shelburne Road, the highway corridor shown at the beginning of the book. Sewer and water lines, highway improvements (public investments), zoning districts and site design regulations (public policies) are drawn on the photograph to show some of the development factors not seen in the physical landscape.[5] The zoning lines reveal the large amount of land dedicated to commercial use. The zone, a tiny area established in 1947, was expanded over time, eventually including over 450 acres, five times more than the area of the nearby downtown. With no obvious limits on space, there was no reason to be economical in the use of land. Sewer and water lines shaped the linear strip pattern, as did the highway itself, which allowed unlimited access from any point along the highway's length.

Every landscape has its hidden framework, and exposing it provides a partial blueprint for development. It can reveal the extent and pattern of future growth. Individuals make land use decisions based on these unseen conditions just as they are influenced by the physical qualities of the land. The developer who, in 1953, subdivided the Shelburne Road orchard into

2.21 Ripe for change. Much of this land in Randolph, Vermont, is zoned for commercial uses such as offices, motels, restaurants, distribution and storage facilities, and industrial parks. This zoning, combined with the sewer line and an I-89 interchange, make change inevitable in this area. The town's regulations mandating low densities and car-friendly site design ensure that new growth will take the form of sprawl.

92 single-family lots was encouraged by residential zoning that allowed the conversion of agricultural land to housing, the prospect of government funded road improvements, and a growing market for large lots. Later, in the 1960s, the new suburbanites who moved to this area created a market that induced businesses to leave downtown Burlington for the cheaper land and brand new infrastructure of the strip. For the many individuals who settled here between 1950 and 1995, the choice was a logical one that offered many benefits, given the development framework. And the framework changed over the years in response to the growth. With pressure from landowners, the town expanded the commercial zone and extended water and sewer lines, providing even more incentive for new development. Transportation policy was a key component of this framework as well. Between 1950 and 1997, the state invested about $32 million in public funds in highway improvements to keep traffic flowing along Shelburne Road. The subsidies eased congestion for a while but ultimately enabled more growth to occur along the corridor, thus causing more congestion. Today another $30 million project is planned to widen the road yet again.

All these changes along Shelburne Road are the result of decisions made by individuals who stood to gain from increased development along the highway, and that development was made possible by an underlying framework of public policy and infrastructure. But as the benefits to individual land and business owners were gained, the costs to the community became clearer. The downtown suffered, the highway was choked with traffic, and the great swath of open land at the edge of town was lost, its

agricultural capacity gone forever.

Understanding the invisible framework makes it possible to predict what any parcel of land might look like in the future. **Figure 2.21** shows the before version of what could become a textbook case of highway sprawl. As with the previous image, some features of the development framework have been made visible.

Much of this land is zoned for commercial uses such as offices, motels, restaurants, distribution and storage facilities, and industrial parks. Here, too, a sewer line runs the length of the state highway within the commercial zone. These factors, combined with the presence of the interstate highway interchange, make this area ripe for change. It has the infrastructure for substantial growth. What that new growth looks like will depend on this town's zoning and site design regulations.

The community's current zoning rules mandate that each parcel be at least five acres and that buildings must not take up more than 20 percent of each lot. As a result, buildings will be isolated on large lots, too far apart to walk between. The regulations also dictate that roads must be 32 feet wide, and, depending on the use, a minimum number of parking spaces will be required for each new development.[6] In effect, these zoning requirements will create a development pattern similar to the commercial strip shown in **Fig. 2.20**, page 20.

2.22 The default setting for growth. This convenience store follows all the rules of contemporary development. When small towns make no changes to the status quo, this is the form that growth typically takes.

To an astute observer, new buildings reveal the underlying development framework of a place and offer hints of what is to come. At the rural intersection in **Fig. 2.22**, the new gas station and convenience store indicates that this land is either unregulated or zoned for commercial use. The building is set back on the lot and surrounded by asphalt, reflecting either local site planning regulations, franchise design standards, or both. The junction of a state highway and a rural collector road provides a steady stream of passersby; the rural location offers less expensive land than the nearby village. Low site costs, easy access, and zoning explain why the mini-mart turned up here. Corporate design templates, local building regulations, and market forces explain why it looks the way it does.

The framework that produces low-density, auto-oriented development is often the default setting for growth in small towns. There are variations on the framework, each with a different end result: Single-family subdivisions, industrial parks, commercial strip highways are a few. But in each case the framework is dictating a type of growth that will slowly consume the productive capability of rural land and deplete its scenic and natural resources.

A DIFFERENT FRAMEWORK

The slow pace of change can contribute to a community drifting toward sprawl, but incremental change is not the cause of it. Incremental change is, in fact, a desirable way to grow. It's the location and form, the pattern of development, that will determine what all the small steps eventually lead to. And the pattern emerges from the framework. The development framework described earlier produced one type of sprawling pattern. But another type of framework can, over time, produce a compact pattern. It can lead individuals to make very different land use choices, creating a very different landscape than the low-density sprawl that seems so inevitable.

This alternative framework, predominant in the 19th century, created dense villages and cities surrounded by open countryside. It provided a structure in which short-term decisions of individual landowners didn't threaten the long-term growth potential of the community. It reserved open land for use by future generations and shaped attractive, strong communities.

To see an example of this framework, take a close look at any small town or village settled in the 18th or 19th centuries. By studying the street, lot, and building pattern at different points in time, you can see the compact pattern emerge.

Bristol, Vermont, is one such place. It began as a crossroads settlement and eventually grew into a village of about 2,000 residents. Its neighborhoods, public buildings, stores, shops, and factories are all within walking distance of the village center (**Fig. 2.23**). Early on, Bristol's founders established the beginnings of a framework when they created a green at the intersection of the two through roads and began to site the community's public buildings around its edges and commercial buildings along one street. With this move, they formed the center around which the town would form itself.

2.23 Bristol, Vermont, began as a crossroads settlement and eventually grew into a village of 2000, accommodating new residents in neighborhoods within walking distance of the central green.

2.24 Bristol in 1871. A local land-holder created two blocks by subdividing the land and building streets, then sold the parcels to individuals who built homes. Source: Beers Atlas.

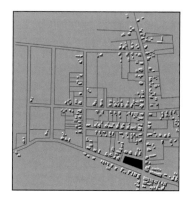

2.25 Bristol in 1889. Five more blocks had been created when the grid was extended and subdivided. Source: Sanborn Maps.

By 1871 (**Fig. 2.24**), a grid of streets had been laid out by a local landholder, forming two new blocks. He built the roads and subdivided the land within the blocks, and then sold the parcels to individuals who built homes. In the following 18 years, as house lots on existing streets filled in, five more blocks were created by extending and subdividing the grid (**Fig. 2.25**). The framework was extended. An 1889 birdseye view of the village shows the unbuilt neighborhood streets, lined with maple trees, awaiting future residents (**Fig. 2.28**). As the village grew, the density increased. It was desirable to live close to the center, with its jobs and services, so parcels near the green were subdivided a second and third time into smaller lots, creating more opportunities for new residences. By 1927, houses had been constructed on the new streets and in empty lots established in the early years. The grid had been expanded again but also filled in. **Figure 2.26** shows the street grid as it exists today. Over the years, every new street fit into an interconnected network, linking each emerging neighborhood with the village center.[7]

The gradual evolution of Bristol is a model of growth without sprawl. Between 1871 (**Fig. 2.27**) and 1889, the town doubled in population. By 1927, it had quadrupled. Newcomers were accommodated at the edge of the settled area in small, efficient lots. But more importantly, new lots were created in the already established neighborhoods by further subdivision of blocks and parcels. This was possible because each new house was placed on the edge of the property, close to the street. This left the interior of the blocks open for new streets. In this way, the village grew without radically expanding its boundaries.

2.26 Bristol in 1927. The town had quadrupled in population. Newcomers were accommodated on small, efficient lots and in subdivided blocks. Source: Sanborn Maps.

2.27 *An altered drawing shows Bristol's 1871 building and street pattern. Source: Beers Atlas, 1871, and Burleigh Birdseye View, 1889. Courtesy University of Vermont.*

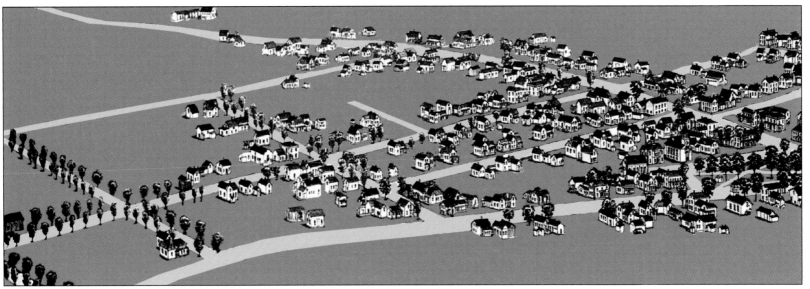

2.28 *This 1889 view shows how new streets and buildings were added over time. Street trees were planted before houses were built. Source: Burleigh Birdseye View, 1889. Courtesy University of Vermont.*

The founders of Bristol created a development framework that accommodated growth in the village for many generations. They had a vision, based on town planning practices of their era, of what the place could become, and they put the physical infrastructure in place to achieve it by creating a center, building an interconnected street network, and establishing building lots. As the town grew, its new residents operated within this overall structure. They bought the lots, constructed homes, and then eventually subdivided their land and sold the lots to newcomers. The slower travel speed dictated by carriages and walking were part of the framework as well. They encouraged people to build as close to the center as possible and maximize the use of their property by siting their houses close to the street.

We can't replicate the development conditions of the 19th century, nor would we necessarily want to. But we can learn a lot from this era, particularly by understanding its sense of the future and its attitude toward land as a limited resource. This can be the key to creating compact, human scale communities that will be valued for generations.

One lesson that could be taken from the 19th century planning book is to take a long view of growth. Look beyond the typical 10- to 20-year time frame to consider the effects of each incremental step on the next 100 years. The public buildings surrounding Bristol's green and the commercial buildings along its Main Street were built to last. The trees planted along the residential streets in 1880 are now huge and stately, lending a grace and beauty to the neighborhood that is missing from contemporary subdivisions where street trees were considered a needless expense. The

early developers of Bristol, like those of so many other 19th century towns across the country, made substantial capital investments in public infrastructure that village residents enjoy today.

The residents of Bristol probably expected that buildings would sit close to the street and close to each other simply because that's the way it was always done. They had a street network and property ownership framework in place that dictated the placement of buildings. Architectural styles came and went over the course of the century, providing a rich diversity in the built environment, but the overall development pattern remained the same. The framework dictated that new streets and neighborhoods would feel like an extension of the village. The grid of streets and sidewalks tied the various components of the village together. It could be extended or subdivided, but it remained interconnected. Incremental change was the norm in 19th century towns. But unlike our era, back then all the small steps led to a coherent whole.

PLANNING AHEAD

Although we tend to think in shorter time spans, contemporary communities can take the long view and look beyond the next few development projects. Some towns have recognized the early warning signs of sprawl evident in small-scale recent growth. They have studied the underlying development framework in their town and imagined what it will produce in the long term. And they have taken steps to change the framework and alter the pattern.

Waitsfield, Vermont, took the long view in 1975, when it weighed the implications of land use controls. The prevailing trend at the time was to zone land along well-traveled roads for commercial uses. But after considering the potential impact of that decision on the town's future landscape, it decided not to employ strip zoning. Instead, it limited businesses to two small areas: the historic village and a second emerging satellite village.

Over the years, the town also used strict zoning controls and the purchase of development rights to prevent farmland along the highway corridor from being converted to house lots (**Fig. 2.30**, page 30). As a result, the highway that runs the length of the town looks much as it did 50 years ago, with farm fields and hedgerows winding for miles along the Mad River Valley (**Fig. 2.29**). In this part of town, Waitsfield achieved its community goal of preserving its traditional settlement pattern of woods and fields surrounding a compact village. It did not prevent or discourage commercial growth. It simply channeled it into a specific area.

2.29 Mad River Valley, 1995.

land in the
floodplain
protected by
easements

floodplain
district

town
boundary

land
protected by
easements

2.30 Invisible framework of farmland protection. Waitsfield
worked with neighboring towns to protect a traditional landscape. Together they used strict zoning controls and the purchase of development rights to prevent farmland along the
highway corridor from being subdivided.

Waitsfield's growth area is highlighted in **Fig. 2.31**. By restricting commercial growth to this one-mile diameter, the town ensured that the flat
arable land along other parts of the corridor would remain free from strip
development.

The town prevented an undesirable outcome by imagining a negative
scenario and rejecting it. Now Waitsfield is working to create a compact
settlement pattern *inside* its new satellite village. Although it had made a
successful effort to remove new development from the highway and contain it within a certain area, the shopping centers, banks, supermarkets,
and stores built there in the past 20 years were spread out and oriented to
the car. As this new commercial center grew, decisions about building
placement and road alignment were made without a clear idea of how
they might all tie together. By the 1990s town planners were ready to alter
the development framework to produce a different result. They didn't
want low-density sprawl. They wanted a compact village, like the historic
one nearby. It was time to remake their "growth area" into something that
resembled a downtown.

They envisioned a dense, lively center with a mix of uses and walkable
streets. They began to put the physical framework in place by planning a
sewage treatment facility and working with landowners and developers to
create a layout of new streets and public spaces. The new plan will dictate
connections within the village and guide the placement of new buildings.
Figure 2.32 depicts a future view of this vision.[8] And they're keeping the
vision in sight as they review new projects. The planning commission

2.31 Commercial growth area. In the 1970s, Waitsfield limited business growth to its historic village (in the upper right) and Irasville, an area of about one square mile (noted here).

2.32 Waitsfield's vision for growth in Irasville. The community developed a plan for new streets, sidewalks, and greens that will serve as the framework when new buildings are constructed.

infill sites

future streets and sidewalks

2.33 Aerial view. Old and new patterns are mixed along one of the main corridors through Manchester, Vermont. New construction in the older village appears in the lower right. The contemporary pattern is evident in the middle of the photo.

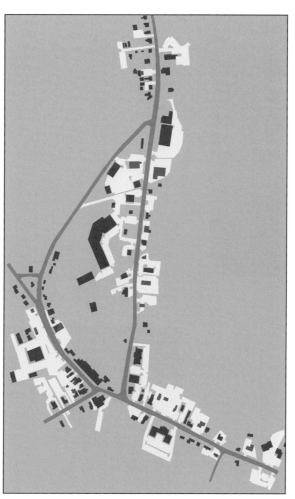

2.34 Existing pattern. This settlement pattern had emerged in Manchester, Vermont, by 1993. Parking lots (in light gray) had spread to fill up the spaces between the smaller, older buildings. New shopping centers were set back from the street.

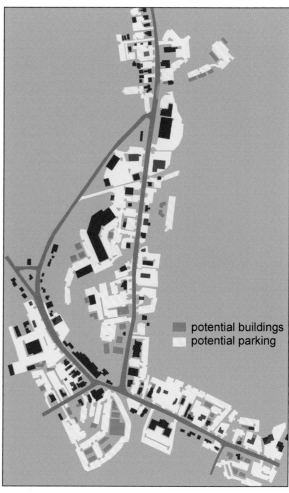

potential buildings
potential parking

2.35 Build-out pattern. This pattern would have emerged if Manchester had kept its car-oriented land use regulations in place. Such regulations would have required large amounts of additional parking to serve the new buildings.

MIGRATIONS TO THE EDGE

Residents of Vergennes, Vermont, have tremendous pride in their small city, with its town green, opera house, and Main Street lined with historic commercial and residential buildings (**Fig. 3.2**). However, changes at the edge of this community have generated some civic debates among city officials, local property owners, businesses, and residents. Out on a major north-south state highway that runs to the east of the city within the adjacent agricultural community of Ferrisburgh, there is a shopping center (**Fig. 3.3**). When the center was first proposed, the City of Vergennes helped out by extending its sewer service to the project. City officials and business people thought the investment would help finance the city's sewer system and promote economic development in the vicinity. At the time, there was little concern that this decision would hurt the downtown. Now the city is struggling to revitalize its downtown in the face of increased competition from this growing commercial area.

The new retail area in Ferrisburgh is changing rapidly. Once part of a sleepy agricultural community with two small villages, it is now becoming a magnet for commercial strip development. Most of the frontage along the state highway is zoned commercial. Shopping centers and convenience stores with gas pumps are gravitating to the highway, and, as a result, shoppers and tourists have less need to venture into the nearby city and village centers. Even the local bus stops at the new shopping area and avoids Vergennes's downtown.

One of the most familiar and cherished images of rural America is a small urban or village settlement surrounded by a landscape of farmland terminating in hills and mountains. However, this image is rapidly becoming a myth of rural life, as one can see from the Ferrisburgh-Vergennes example. As more and more people settle in the open spaces surrounding these centers, they attract shops and services to serve them and let the towns cope with vacant buildings and declining jobs and sales. With time it becomes difficult even to find the edge of the settled area, as the boundaries of town and countryside blur.

While many old settlements retained their compact form during decades of growth, the newer developments of the post-World War II period introduced a different pattern affecting both rural lands and urban centers. This sprawl pattern of low-density, auto-oriented development began at the edge of urban and village centers but gradually leapfrogged out into more rural settings. Back in the downtowns, buildings were razed and suburban-style projects were introduced in an effort to meet the demands of consumers and businesses.

Many communities are now rejecting sprawl and choosing instead the compact, historic settlement patterns as a better way to grow. These communities have revitalized their downtowns, added new compact neighborhoods, and taken steps to protect the open spaces surrounding the built-up areas. They are keeping alive the tradition of rural development: compact settled areas separated by open countryside.

For many small towns, the first wave of peripheral development began in the 1950s when subdivisions began to appear at the edge of urban centers. With increased use of the automobile and dramatic improvements to

3.2 City officials in Vergennes, Vermont, extended sewer service to a shopping center in a neighboring town, putting downtown Vergennes at a disadvantage.

3.3 This shopping center, located along a major state highway in the rural farming town of Ferrisburgh, Vermont, may become the first step in a strip development.

roads, lands that once were inaccessible to development became potential sites for growth. Projects leapfrogged well past the existing boundaries of the developed areas out into farm fields. This haphazard pattern left large gaps of open land, including actively used crop land, where pressures built over time for similar conversions.

Over a 30- to 40-year period St. Albans Town, Vermont, followed the path of many other rural places, becoming the regional center for growth, while nearby St. Albans City languished (**Fig. 3.5**, area 1). Initially, open spaces right on the edge of St. Albans City were subdivided into small house lots (**Fig. 3.5**, area 2). Later, large lot residential subdivisions—reflecting the desires of families for more privacy—leapfrogged out into agricultural areas in the St. Albans Town (**Fig. 3.5**, area 3). Soon offices and industries followed the out-migration, developing on large lots with plenty of space for parking, away from the city center. Between 1970 and 1996, population in the city declined by 5.6 percent while that in the town grew by 69.5 percent.

Statewide data from Vermont in **Fig. 3.4** illustrate that traditional urban and village centers are losing their role as growth centers while suburban communities gain the majority of the state's new population. Population growth was measured in urban and village centers, surrounding suburban communities, rural communities, and resort towns.[1] Between 1950 and 1990, nearly 60 percent of all population growth took place in the suburban communities, while only 11 percent took place in the urban and village centers. Clearly, the population centers of the state have begun to shift from urban and village centers to the suburbs.

3.4 Share of Vermont State Population Growth by Type of Community, 1950-1990

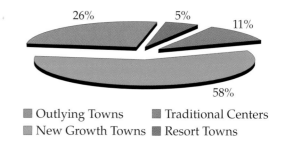

26%   5%   11%

58%

■ Outlying Towns   ■ Traditional Centers
■ New Growth Towns   ■ Resort Towns

3.5 Initially, open spaces on the edge of the City of St. Albans, Vermont, were subdivided into small house lots (1). Later, large lot residential subdivisions leapfrogged out into farming areas in the Town of St. Albans (2). Offices and industries followed, built on large lots with plenty of space for parking far from the city center (3).

COMPETITION BETWEEN EDGES AND CENTERS

The movement of retail stores to outlying locations closely followed the residential growth in fringe areas. One shopping center developer from Burlington, Vermont, said in 1962, "We know that the city's main growth will go south because of the healthy conditions there. It has a young population average, large new commercial centers, desirable residential developments and is easy of access to out of town shoppers."[2]

Properties were cheaper at the edge than in the downtown (**Fig. 3.6**). They also offered more space for extensive parking lots and the large, one-story stores that national retailers were promoting. Accessibility seemed ideal on a major highway leading from the downtown or adjacent to a highway interchange. Suburban towns also wanted the new commercial growth to boost their tax base and keep property taxes low. This perceived benefit to growth fostered competition between communities for commercial development.

As towns competed for growth, those on the outskirts gradually claimed larger and larger shares of the retail market. In Chittenden County, Vermont, retail sales in Burlington (**Fig. 3.7**), the traditional regional core, declined by 36 percent over 20 years while sales in other communities in the county grew 500 percent (**Fig. 3.8**). The decline in Burlington occurred despite the substantial investment of both public and private funds in downtown improvements between 1986 and 1998.[3]

The loss of retail sales in urban and village centers has affected property values and employment. While suburban communities' commercial property values have soared, those in urban centers have either declined

3.6 Six miles from downtown Burlington, Vermont, new commercial growth has emerged at Taft Corners, formerly a rural crossroad.

3.8 Retail Sales Trends, Burlington, VT

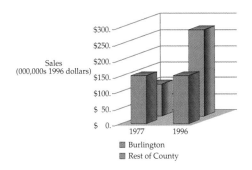

Sales
(000,000s 1996 dollars)

$300.
$250.
$200.
$150.
$100.
$ 50.
$ 0.

1977   1996

■ Burlington
■ Rest of County

3.7 A historic pattern of compact commercial growth in downtown Burlington.

or increased by only a small amount due to vacancies. Retail employment has also dropped in many cities. Locally owned businesses have shut their doors or moved to lower rent locations in the face of competition from national and regional chain stores in outlying suburban towns.

Around the country in small cities and towns, rows of vacant storefronts and empty upper floors demonstrate the effects of the downtowns' loss of retail sales to the edges. These images seem to show that these places have lost in the competition for commercial development. Nevertheless, some communities have managed to salvage their downtowns by foresight and planning. In Burlington, efforts were made in the 1970s to build a marketplace and transit center in the downtown and to fight the malls and big boxes on the periphery while the marketplace established itself as a retail center. The Church Street Marketplace today is one of the nation's few successful auto-free pedestrian malls.

3.9 Downtown Montpelier, Vermont, began to lose its role as a regional retail center in the 1970s. The culprits: strip development and development at an interstate highway interchange.

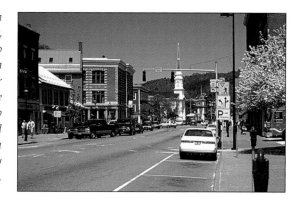

3.10 In the 1960s, farmland along this road was paved over for a shopping center.

3.11 In the town of Berlin, outside Montpelier, this interchange, built in 1970, is now the site of a regional shopping mall anchored by a Wal-Mart.

3.12 Retail sales once consolidated in the downtowns of Barre City and Montpelier are now spread out over four locations. Three are shown here.

In Central Vermont, retail sales formerly were concentrated in the downtowns of Montpelier (**Fig. 3.9**) and Barre, where people lived, shopped, and worked. Today four shopping areas compete: the two downtowns, a strip highway area (**Fig. 3.10**), and the interstate interchange area in the Town of Berlin (**Fig. 3.11**). Each of these areas requires continuing public and private investment—in roads and traffic management, stormwater management, parking, public utilities and services, and building maintenance and improvement. The market isn't big enough for all four to thrive, and the impacts of this growth are showing, especially in the older strip commercial area and in one of the downtowns.

Montpelier's downtown is typical of many small regional centers in rural areas (**Fig. 3.12**, area 1). Shops and businesses line the main streets. Offices and apartments are located above the stores. Many people live in residential neighborhoods that are within walking distance of the town center. In the 1950s and 1960s, concerns arose about the effects of the increased use of automobiles in these communities. Parking was hard to find in the town centers, the narrow streets were congested, and space was too limited for the needs of growing retail stores.

In the 1960s the rich farmland of a river valley in Berlin was paved over for a strip center of retail shops (**Fig. 3.11**). The new center with its large parking lot located directly off a major state highway was very accessible to the increasing number of shoppers who were using their cars. In time most of the highway became lined with auto dealers, discount stores, muffler shops, fast food restaurants and more strip centers (**Fig. 3.12**, area 2).

The highway was widened and traffic signals were added to improve the flow of cars between retail developments and nearby communities.

Upon the completion of the interstate highway in 1970, a nearby interchange began to attract growth (**Fig. 3.12**, area 3). Following the opening of a hospital, a motel, and some offices, a controversial regional shopping mall was proposed in the early 1980s. Despite heated debates in the permit process about its environmental and economic impacts, the mall was approved and built.

Within a few years, other retailers in the area began to feel the impact of the mall. An anchor store in a shopping center out on the older commercial strip went out of business, which led to other retailers closing their doors. A large, locally owned discount store also closed. There were vacancies in a nearby downtown. In the mid-1990s, a local developer undertook a major renovation of one of the strip centers. This attracted new tenants and generated hope that the area could be revived. Then Wal-Mart announced plans to take over a section of the regional mall vacated by a department store, and new concerns arose about how the nation's number one retailer would affect existing businesses.

With four regional shopping centers and with limited economic expansion, competition is fierce in this small area. Both historic centers participate in the state's downtown program to take advantage of tax and other incentives for growth. Berlin recently developed a master plan for the redesign of its strip commercial area. If these efforts pay off, more businesses and shoppers may return from the edge back to the older centers.

3.13 *A major industry moves its main facility to a highway on the edge of the town of Arlington, Vermont.*

3.14 *A historic industrial building along a tree-lined street in Springfield, Vermont.*

SOWING JOBS IN GREEN FIELDS

An industry in the Town of Arlington was seeking plenty of land and easy access to highways when it found a rural site. The new site had a large open area and was located just off a limited access state highway. The industry had looked into expanding its operations within the village of Arlington, but was unable to find sufficient space for its needs. Although it still maintains some of its business in the village, a major portion of its operations are now out at this highway location (**Fig. 3.13**). This case points out a major challenge for small towns: how to accommodate the growing and changing needs of industries within compact community centers.

Older industrial buildings in urban centers are usually multi-storied and close to residential neighborhoods and commercial centers. The industrial building in **Fig. 3.14** is located along an urban street. While this building is now awaiting rehabilitation and new tenants, in the past sidewalks enabled employees to walk to nearby businesses and homes. These traditional patterns offer models for new industrial growth within or adjacent to compact settlements.

Industrial activity often follows the residential and commercial growth to the edge of town centers. This increases the number of jobs in suburban areas, sometimes at the expense of jobs in the centers. In Vermont, 46 percent of the state's job growth between 1980 and 1996 took place in suburban communities. Even rural towns gained a larger share (26 percent) of jobs than the traditional urban and village centers (21 percent) (**Fig. 3.15**). Older centers have a hard time retaining existing businesses or attracting new ones because they must compete with the lower

3.15 Share of Vermont State Employment Growth, by Type of Community, 1980-1996

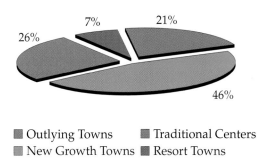

■ Outlying Towns   ■ Traditional Centers
■ New Growth Towns   ■ Resort Towns

land values and open spaces of outlying areas.

But industries also face growing problems when they migrate to rural areas. Employees don't always like the longer commuting times and isolation from services and restaurants out in remote locations. Affordable housing is often hard to find there. More and more industries and business groups are reconsidering urban locations or are trying to create mixed-use environments around their sites. (See Chapter 5 for more discussion.)

In the 1980s the small community of Richford ran out of space for industrial development in its compact downtown and turned to the green fields of the surrounding landscape for a site for a new industrial park. Although the community once thrived on agriculture and some manufacturing, jobs had declined and local officials wanted to attract more employment to the town. With the help of a regional industrial group, a 23-acre site was found about two miles outside the village. The town extended water and sewer service out to the site, and within three years the park had its first tenant (**Fig. 3.16**). Today, there is one major business in the park providing vitally needed jobs for residents. Nine acres are still available for more development. In the summer of 2000 a local entrepreneur announced that his family would rehabilitate an empty building on the road to the park for a service center that would house a day care center, a fitness center, and other businesses. Meanwhile, in the village center, commercial and industrial buildings are boarded up and the search is on for new tenants.

In the 1970s and 1980s, many small communities were making plans for

3.16 A new 23-acre industrial park on a state highway two miles outside the village of Richford.

3.17 *Historic Richford Village with vacant industrial buildings in the center along the river.*

industrial parks like the one in Richford. The parks featured large lots, low prefabricated buildings, little or no landscaping, broad building setbacks, wide roads, and ample paved areas for parking and loading. From an economic standpoint, low land prices and abundant open space made compact patterns of development unnecessary. Little attention was given to employees who did not drive or own cars, preserving the character of the open land around the village, offering shops and services that workers could walk to at lunch time, or reusing older structures in the village.

The historic pattern of industrial development in the Village of Richford stands in sharp contrast to the new park on the periphery. Multi-story industrial, masonry buildings line the main street and the river in the heart of the downtown (**Fig. 3.17**, page 49). There is no on-site parking for these buildings; employees could use nearby parking lots or walk from their homes.

Recently, a furniture manufacturer vacated these masonry buildings, removing 20 jobs from the town. It is at this point that many communities would give up on their in-town industrial buildings and focus their efforts on more modern industrial parks outside of town centers. This community did not. While the buildings pictured here are still vacant, the community is trying to find new uses for them. Strong citizen concern for the downtown was revealed during a community visioning process. The town resolved to do something about the vacant and underused buildings. To follow up on the community vision, a strategic plan was developed and architects were hired to assess the rehabilitation needs of the historic struc-

tures. In 2000, an investor bought the buildings, and a local group has organized to advocate for the revitalization of their downtown.

Richford Town and Richford Village have pursued economic development on two fronts—in the village and at the industrial park. Both efforts have met with mediocre success. There are vacant lots at the park and vacant buildings in the village. The new service center threatens to make village redevelopment even more difficult. The decision to develop the park seemed like a good idea in the 1980s, but today this leapfrog development consumes valuable open space with unremarkable buildings while significant historic commercial and industrial buildings sit idle in the village. In the long run, that decision may have been made at the expense of community vitality. The town and village are fortunate to have a dedicated group of citizens and business people who are working hard to overcome this dilemma.

CHANGES IN THE CENTERS

Cities and towns in rural America have had to adapt to the automobile, cope with traffic congestion, meet the demands of businesses for larger and more prominent spaces, clean up contaminated sites, and provide safe and sanitary housing and social services for residents, especially in the aftermath of World War II. These communities also have had to adjust to the shift of people, shops, and services to outlying communities.

Initially, the responses to these demands in small cities and towns produced only minor alterations in the traditional urban form. Parking spaces were arranged along streets and in the back of lots. Traffic controls were introduced so vehicles could safely make their way to and through the centers. Roads were widened to accommodate cars and trucks. When buildings were burned or razed, they were replaced with bigger structures for department stores, banks, and public services.

Over time, the changes to cities became more pronounced. Vacancies on Main Street began to blight the downtown (**Fig. 3.18**). Major road and parking projects caused the demolition of many buildings and created wide gaps between neighborhoods. Low-income and elderly people became increasingly isolated in older neighborhoods. With shops and services locating at the edges of cities and small towns, residents traveled farther to shop. Open space receded as development consumed the nearby landscape.

Urban renewal was one of the most significant physical changes that occurred within cities and villages. This national program was initiated in 1949 to enable cities to declare certain areas "blighted" and then to make

3.18 A vacant department store in downtown Pittsfield, Massachusetts.

3.19 Street pattern before urban renewal.

alterations to these areas with financial assistance from the federal government. When urban renewal was prevalent during the 1950s and 1960s, planning and design practitioners favored clearance of tightly built-up areas, especially those with health and safety problems and concentrations of poverty. Residents of these areas were often relocated into public housing. Some old neighborhoods were replaced with tall, modern buildings surrounded by large empty spaces. Streets were severed. Idealistic plans for new development frequently included large commercial buildings, luxury apartments, hotels and public buildings—visions that were far from the economic realities of these small towns.

In the 1960s, six blocks of Burlington, Vermont, were consolidated into one 19-acre parcel (**Fig. 3.19**). Eight acres of east-west and north-south streets were eliminated to make way for an urban renewal project (**Figs. 3.20 and 3.21**). Small residential and commercial properties were replaced by large blocks of buildings containing a hotel, shopping mall, banks, offices, and a parking garage. Recently, some upper income condominiums were added to the site. A major department store and a second parking garage were constructed in 1998 on a portion of the remaining land.

While many of these uses are desirable for the downtown, the pattern and form of the development has destroyed the pedestrian environment and street life of this area. The elimination of streets has made access through the downtown difficult for vehicles, bicycles, and pedestrians. It has also wiped out a cohesive neighborhood of low- and moderate-income housing close to city shops and services.

3.20 Street pattern after urban renewal.

3.21 Burlington's urban renewal area erases part of the street network, creating large areas for development.

3.22 Intersection in Morrisville, Vermont, in the early 1900s. Source: Vermont Historical Society.

3.23 The same Morrisville intersection in 1998.

Nationally, many small cities and towns were subjected to urban renewal with ugly and disruptive results. However, these undesirable new developments woke people up, and a period of preservation and enhancement of remaining assets in downtowns followed. Nevertheless, there are still communities that tear down blocks of urban buildings in an effort to assemble parcels and attract national retailers and other businesses to their downtowns.

Other forms of suburban development that have made their way into downtowns and village centers are the strip mall and gas station/convenience store. These projects are designed to make it easier for motorists to get to stores and services. Such auto-oriented projects have, however, interrupted the pattern of buildings lining streets and the pedestrian flow along sidewalks while injecting designs incompatible with historic districts.

Some urban street corners have been dramatically altered by the destruction of historic buildings. In many cases they have been replaced with large expanses of paved areas hosting gas pumps and convenience stores. In the village of Morrisville, Vermont, a historic hotel was once the focal point of an intersection in the heart of the village (**Fig. 3.22**, page 53). Today, a gas station with a mini-mart sits at this prime site (**Fig. 3.23**, page 53). Garish lighting and signage, huge canopies dwarfing the small gas pumps, and extensive paving conflict with the surrounding modest, two-story buildings that have no provision for automobiles save a few parking spaces out front.

In the City of St. Albans, Vermont—a short distance from historic commercial buildings—a large parking lot in front of a strip center lines Main Street (**Fig. 3.24**). Wide driveways allow easy auto access into the development. Shops are set way back from the street edge in a long, single-story building (**Fig. 3.25**). Instead of strolling by a row of commercial buildings and peering into store windows, as they would do in the historic town center, pedestrians cannot even see shop windows from the street. The development is disconnected from the street life of the city.

Strip commercial centers within downtown areas have created auto-dominated, isolated places that discourage pedestrian traffic. While people in the rest of the downtown make their way to a wide range of shops and services on foot after parking their cars in a central location, shoppers at the strip center drive their cars in to do their business at a few shops and then leave. Both the gas stations and the strip centers are typically one-story, single-use buildings set off in their own enclaves. They offer a strong contrast to the multi-story mixed use buildings of stone, brick, and clapboard oriented to public streets in the downtowns.

Many small cities and towns in rural areas have invested huge amounts of time and money fighting off the decline in their centers, often with limited results. Today many of these places realize that imitating the building patterns of the suburbs is unproductive and has caused them to lose their unique character—their architecture, history, pedestrian environment, and diversity of activities. Now they are rethinking their approach and looking for ways to capitalize on these assets.

3.24 *A parking lot and strip center along Main Street in St. Albans City, Vermont.*

3.25 *Aerial view of a commercial strip center on Main Street in St. Albans City, Vermont.*

3.26 *Suburban sites are attractive to developers because land is cheaper there, they have room to expand, and they can provide on-site parking and highway access.*

3.27 *Downtown properties can be difficult to develop; problems include high land values, lack of parking space, and the presence of hazardous materials.*

NEW PATTERNS OF URBAN GROWTH

Communities are looking for ways to expand their urban centers without sacrificing their historic character. By creating incentives for downtown development, finding new uses for old buildings, filling the gaps in the urban fabric, and strengthening pedestrian life, many cities and towns have made this happen.

Local officials and citizens are working to establish urban growth boundaries and green belts on the edges of these centers to stem the relentless tide of sprawling development. In these communities a complex mixture of zoning techniques, public investment strategies, and purchase and donation of conservation easements are used to accomplish these goals.

Many people involved with development in both town centers and edge locations say that the higher cost of doing business downtown is one of the major reasons that these places are losing development opportunities. Some businesses like the benefits of a downtown location, such as access to financial institutions, other businesses, cultural events, and shops and services, and are willing to pay the higher costs. But others prefer to locate in open spaces on the edge where driving and parking are easier, land is cheaper, and there is room to grow (**Fig. 3.26**).

Costs can run higher in downtowns because of permitting complexities, site and building conditions such as hazardous materials, development difficulties, and high land values. Developers and business people are also concerned about finding adequate parking and good highway access in downtowns (**Fig. 3.27**).

To counter these disadvantages, municipalities and states around the

3.28 Community support and public funds enabled renovation of a large historic building into housing and offices in the village of Waterbury, Vermont.

3.29 Formerly home to a printing company, this building now houses several small businesses.

country are creating incentives for downtown development, including tax abatements, financial aid to clean up contaminated sites, special codes for historic structures, streamlined permitting, and priority access to state grants and loans.

In the village of Waterbury, Vermont (**Fig. 3.28**), public funds and community support led to the renovation of a large, historic building with retail and office space on the first floor and low- and moderate-income rental apartments upstairs. This project has not only brought to life what was a large, empty eyesore in the heart of the village, but it has also spawned other revitalization efforts and new businesses on nearby properties.

While many buildings in large cities were demolished in the 1960s, 1970s, and 1980s, some rural communities and small towns fortunately escaped the wholesale destruction of historic buildings in their centers. As a result, many recent downtown redevelopment projects have retained mixed use space in historic compact forms. The rehabilitation of historic buildings has the added benefit of using existing resources and infrastructure.

When a Burlington, Vermont, printing company decided to relocate from an urban site to a rural farming area, it left vacant a block-long building in an established commercial and industrial area. The building was renovated with smaller spaces for multiple businesses and today is fully occupied (**Fig. 3.29**).

In Winooski, Vermont, homes, businesses, and streets were demolished in the 1970s, leaving a huge gap between a mill and the remainder of the downtown (**Figs. 3.30 and 3.31**, page 58). This gap was paved over for a sur-

3.30 *Downtown Winooski before urban renewal. Source: Dan Higgins.*

3.31 *In the 1970s, the center of the city of Winooski was demolished and a parking lot put in its place.*

3.32 Now Winooski plans to bring back a compact, high-density, mixed-use center. Source: Truex, Cullins, and Partners.

face parking lot. The historic mill was spared and converted to a retail mall and office space. For the past decade the city has been struggling to find new uses for the parking lot in order to knit the downtown back together. Now the city has an ambitious new plan to fill this void and is gaining support from the state and federal governments.

The new plan (**Fig. 3.32**) proposes to set aside 104 acres along the Winooski River for public recreation and a natural area while redeveloping the remaining 21 acres. The 156,000-square-foot historic Champlain Mill will be renovated for mixed commercial and public uses. New office, government, hotel, entertainment, and retail space will be made available on the former parking lot. A large parking garage will be built underground. Homes for 800 households are planned along the river and above retail stores. Once built, the project will reinvigorate the downtown, protect important river frontage, reduce dependence on automobiles, and provide new homes.

Often people think there is no room to grow in urban areas—that these places are filled up and that raw land must be found in outlying areas. However, cities often have many spots that get overlooked. Cities are dynamic places. Within them, buildings and industries vacate outmoded space; structures get torn down or burn down, freeing up land. Vacant lots can be filled and empty buildings rehabilitated. By filling in, building up, and redeveloping existing properties, cities can grow within their boundaries.

In the small state capital of Montpelier, Vermont, two new commercial buildings and an affordable housing apartment complex have provided

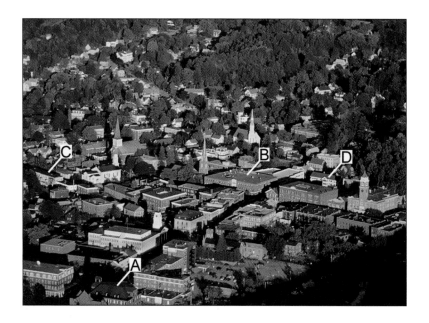

3.33 Four infill projects in the city of Montpelier: A mixed-use, multi-story office building (A); a new commercial building and parking facility in the heart of downtown (B); newly built and renovated apartments (C); and a new commercial building (D).

3.34 Renovated riverfront apartments offer clean and attractive affordable housing in Montpelier. (Also Fig. 3.33-C.)

3.35 On State Street, a new building housing a bank and state offices replaced a single-story structure. (Also Fig. 3.33-A.)

3.36 A new residential and commercial building in the village center of Hardwick, Vermont, replaces a structure demolished by fire.

models for infill development. Across from the state capitol, a four-story office building replaced a low-rise building that only used a small portion of its lot (**Figs. 3.33**, Site A, and **Fig. 3.35**). At a central downtown intersection, a new three-story building was constructed on a site where a fire had destroyed several buildings. There are retail uses on the first floor and offices upstairs. At the back of the building is a multi-story parking garage (**Fig. 3.33**, Site B). Along the river running through the downtown, several dismal cinderblock apartment buildings were replaced with attractive, affordable housing units (**Fig. 3.33**, Site C, and **Fig. 3.34**). A new multi-story office building provides space for nonprofit organizations and downtown businesses within walking distance of the state capitol **Fig. 3.33**, Site D).

A fire in the historic village of Hardwick (**Fig. 3.36**) left families and businesses homeless. A new building that respected the traditional pattern of development along the street was constructed on the site with federal and state assistance. The village gained attractive and safe affordable housing units and first floor commercial space.

A series of fires in the early 1990s severely damaged five landmark buildings in Randolph village (**Fig. 3.37**). A temporary building was constructed for the local variety store while reconstruction was under way. State and federal funds were obtained for senior housing on the upper floors of one historic building. To receive these public benefits and to meet local zoning rules, developers made the new designs compatible with the historic streetscape. The result has been a resurgence of interest in revitalizing the village center and greater public involvement in local government.

3.37 New mixed-use buildings replace burnt out structures in downtown Randolph, Vermont.

ESTABLISHING A GREEN BELT

One way to stop the gradual creep of sprawl out from town centers into the countryside is to establish a green belt—an edge of connected open space that is clearly defined and protected for the long term. Green belts reinforce the places they encircle as the prime locations for development.

To establish a green belt, a community must first have a clear vision about where it wants to grow and what lands it wants to preserve. Once the vision is established and desired open space areas are defined, the community can determine which open spaces can be linked into a green belt around the built-up areas of the town.

Most communities find they must use a variety of tools in order to protect a green belt. Typically, these tools include zoning and subdivision regulations, acquisition of land, purchase or donation of conservation easements, and water and sewer service containment policies. Zoning regulations often contain special provisions for the protection of greenbelts. Examples include transfer of development rights, clustering, or overlay districts. Standards in subdivision regulations can insure that the greenbelt is not broken up. Acquiring land and easements is the safest way to protect a green belt over the long run. Many states offer cost sharing for such acquisitions, and many local governments set aside funds for this purpose. Some landowners may be interested in donating conservation easements in return for tax benefits.

The rural community of Charlotte, Vermont, began to protect its green belt in the 1960s, when the first in a series of regulations limiting development along a major state highway was established (**Fig. 3.38**). This fore-sight resulted in the maintenance of agriculture along a scenic stretch of the highway for many years. Eventually, however, the pressures of suburban development in the community began to threaten the area with large lot developments. A local philanthropist grew concerned that this exceptional resource would be lost and took steps to acquire some properties in the area. Nearly 15 years later, over 800 acres of land have been protected with help from this private citizen, a local land trust, the Vermont Housing and Conservation Board, local citizens, and a national conservation group. Now the land contains a farm, a community park with trails and scenic overlooks, and wide expanses of permanently conserved open space. The strip development that had been creeping down the state highway from other communities will stop at Charlotte's green belt.

There is hope that the lines between centers and the countryside can become more distinct in the future. Public policies that promote downtown development and reuse of historic structures may lead to more building activity in central areas. Redesigning urban renewal to work for today's needs, as the City of Winooski is proposing, may introduce an era of community building, not community demolition, in town centers. Infill development is already experiencing a resurgence in urban centers as communities, property owners, and developers find opportunities to expand existing buildings, fill in vacant lots, and rehabilitate older structures. At the same time, work must continue on the edges to protect important open spaces, preserve important natural resources, and provide residents with recreation opportunities within walking distance of neighborhoods.

3.38 With the help of private investors and government funds, the community of Charlotte, Vermont, has protected several parcels of land to create a greenbelt along a state highway at the edge of town.

NOTES

1. Vermont Forum on Sprawl and the Center for Rural Studies at the
   University of Vermont. Burlington, Vermont, 1999.

2. *Burlington Free Press*, April 1962.

3. Elizabeth Humstone and Thomas Muller. "Economic and Fiscal Impacts
   of Proposed Filene's Department Store, " for Burlington, Vermont, 1997.

THE FRAGMENTED PATTERN

Ask a small child to trace and cut some shapes out of paper and he will inevitably begin in the middle. Although there may be room on the sheet to trace several carefully arranged shapes, the child won't grasp this. His instinct is to center the template, trace and cut, then ask for a second sheet of paper to create a second shape. In the process, he'll generate a pile of scraps.

You can see a similar phenomenon occurring at highway interchanges (**Fig. 4.2**). Like many such interstate interchanges, this area was developed recently, in a low-density, auto-oriented pattern. After the buildings, roads, and parking lots are cut out of the picture, only scattered pieces of open land remain. As a pattern, it looks as if a child with scissors has been at work. The leftover woods and fields aren't big enough to farm, to hike in, or to provide shelter for many animals. Certainly, the economic benefit of this development has been great. But it wasn't necessary to sacrifice natural resources to achieve this benefit. If the land had been used more efficiently, if the same offices, stores and schools were located closer together, you would see a different pattern, with large chunks of open land and fewer small fragments.

Fragmentation is the process of carving up large tracts of land into smaller pieces, forming a patchwork of developed and open land. It occurs on cropland at the edge of small towns, on the wooded hillsides of resort areas—wherever families or businesses seek cheaper, more private, or more scenic rural places to inhabit. Across the country, our contemporary settlement patterns are nibbling away at the forests, fields, wetlands, and shorelines of rural areas.

The small-scale, incremental nature of change, so typical of rural towns, is one reason open land is vulnerable. As illustrated in an earlier chapter, the inability to see the process of change— to imagine the future and take steps to avoid undesirable and unintended consequences—is one reason large chunks of open land dwindle to smaller fragments. This chapter will focus on other factors: regulations, local investments in roads, water and sewer lines, and a deeply rooted desire in many Americans for a piece of rural life. It will also show how fragmentation of land affects both the agricultural landscape and the natural environment of rural areas, and how communities can alter their development patterns to avoid fragmentation.

4.2 *As is true at many other highway interchanges, recent development around a Colchester, Vermont, interchange resulted in a low-density, auto-oriented pattern. When the buildings, roads, and parking lots are cut out of the picture, only scattered pieces of open land remain.*

LOVING THE COUNTRY TO PIECES

In 1911, when the horse, the train, and the trolley dominated the nation's transportation system and the vast majority of Americans lived close together in compact communities, Herbert Ladd Towle, a writer for *Harper's Weekly*, wondered what it would be like if the automobile, then in the hands of a few elite, were made available to every man "of moderate means." It would be glorious, he suggested, for those living within a one-mile radius of a train station, to break free of "the zone of common demand, fixed by the leg power of the hoi-polloi," and be able to own a home in the country. "If every business man could have an inexpensive mechanical horse which could carry him three or four miles from house to station in fifteen minutes," he wrote, "and if by going that distance he could have a real farm with apples and chickens and fresh milk, for less than the price he pays now for a house and a lot at the end of a fifteen minute walk, wouldn't he think pretty hard before he turned down the farm?" Towle had a vision of a new America in which the choicest pastoral land is made available for home sites. He urged his readers not to be "blinded by an obsession that civilized beings are only found within five minutes of a trolley line," and to consider seeking out "fresh air, sunshine, and green things."[1]

Towle was making an assumption that city dwellers of the time felt a strong urge to escape to a more rural lifestyle. Given the opportunity, he reasoned, Americans would choose to live in the country. It would take 40 years, but history proved him right. In the 1950s, when automobiles finally became available to the masses, Towles's vision of a countryside inhabited by the middle class began to come true. During the second half of the century, Americans moved from cities to suburbs. At the turn of the 21st century, the exodus continues, this time from the suburbs to the countryside, completing the "revolution" Towles had imagined 90 years earlier. Population in nonmetropolitan areas grew three times faster in the 1990s than it did a decade earlier, with the nation's most rural areas, the Mountain West, the Upper Great Lakes, the Ozarks, and rural areas of the Northeast, seeing the fastest growth.[2] The Sierra Nevada region of California doubled in population between 1970 and 1990, and is expected to double again by 2020. Its rural landscape, wild lands, and open spaces appeal to newcomers, who are choosing to locate there rather than in other areas of California.[3] Just as the automobile freed Americans from the confines of the city, the completion of the interstate highway system and the more recent increase in telecommuting have released them from the suburbs.

It is easy to find evidence of this demographic trend in small towns across the country. Newcomers typically arrive from some more built-up place in search of a rural lifestyle. A 1998 study of recent homebuyers by the Maine State Planning Office found only 12 percent move to or stay in in-town settings; 42 percent move outward to suburban or rural settings, and another 33 percent already in these settings stay there.[4] One couple in the Rocky Mountains that has followed this urge to live at the shifting edge between the countryside and suburbia was interviewed in a recent *Denver Post* article about sprawl in Colorado. After relocating from

RURAL HOMES AND FARMLAND

Southern California to a Denver suburb in 1982, they made a second move in 1993 to a then rural county. Six years later, unhappy with the changing landscape of the now suburban town, they are exchanging their hilltop subdivision home for a ranch in a more remote area of the state. "Colorado Springs was becoming so congested. We wanted to breathe..." the wife said. "We wanted acreage and no neighbors, at least not right out the front door. To be in the mountains. Living in the pines." Although they acknowledge that their moves have contributed to the problem they want to escape, they insist on exercising their right to choose a rural home, saying, "but that's what America is all about. Freedom of choice where you want to live."[5]

In many regions of the country, land is being developed faster than the rate at which the population is growing. We're living, working, and shopping in bigger buildings, occupying larger lots, and traveling farther to get there. And in the process of spreading out, we're having a dramatic effect on the rural areas we seek out.

While Americans may be moving out to the country, they're not especially interested in working the land. According to the National Resources Inventory of the U.S. Department of Agriculture, 16 million acres of cropland, forestland, and open space were converted to urban and other uses between 1992 and 1997. This loss represents an annual rate of 3.2 million acres per year, up from the rate of 1.4 million acres per year between 1982 and 1992.[6] In farm communities where growth rates are high, agricultural land gets subdivided into house lots, breaking up large, tillable parcels into smaller, less usable pieces.

The newcomers have different needs, different attitudes, and a very different relationship to the land than the farmers or ranchers they're replacing. Those moving into rural areas typically have more interest in the picturesque qualities of the land than its productive capability. This often makes it difficult for farming and contemporary development to coexist. New homes are set not on the edge of arable land but in the center. Driveways bisect fields, interrupting farming operations (**Fig. 4.3**, page 70). As suburban development creeps into agricultural areas, the basic elements of the working farm often are not maintained.

The process of agricultural fragmentation can be made clearer by looking at how land is divided when development occurs. **Figure 4.4** (see page 71) is a simulated view of how Jericho, Vermont, looked in 1937, when most of the land was used for agriculture. Buildings were located in clusters at farmsteads, crossroad hamlets, or in the village, set very close to the road. This practice kept large tracts of land open for farming, with a few

4.3 In Dorset, Vermont, new houses are set not at the edge of this arable farmland but in the center. Driveways bisect fields, interrupting farming operations.

4.4 *A simulated view of agricultural patterns in Jericho, Vermont, circa 1937. Source: University of Vermont Department of Geography.*

steeper areas reserved for wood production. Over the years these tracts were sold and divided into smaller parcels to create house lots. By 1995, the pattern of property ownership had changed radically (**Fig. 4.5**). Very few of the large, tillable parcels remained.

Since the production of food and fiber is no longer locally based, does it really matter that farms have been replaced by housing subdivisions? To communities that view agricultural soil as a valuable natural resource to be preserved for future generations, it does. Agriculture represents not only an important way of life and a source of valuable open space but also the opportunity for growing and producing food and fiber. Food security is becoming a global issue. The ability to meet the food supply demands of a dramatically growing world population is threatened by the loss of arable farmland in countries that will be most in need. As the global demands on U.S. food producers grow, a reliable local source of food and fiber will be increasingly important. Farmland also contains valuable natural resources, including wetlands, wildlife habitat, and buffers to water bodies. Well-managed farmland helps to preserve these critical community resources.

Farming is a way of life in many rural towns. It provides jobs, contributes to the local economy, and creates demand for support businesses, such as equipment sales and grain supplies. Local agriculture supports "value-added" products, such as cheese, ice cream, cider, and syrup. Many rural areas of the country depend on the scenic beauty created by open pastureland, cultivated cropland, and managed woodland to attract

4.5 *Actual view of housing subdivisions on the same land in 1995.*

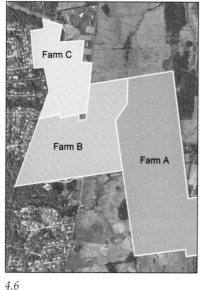

4.6

4.7

4.8

4.9

4.10

4.6 and 4.7 In the 1950s and '60s, two farm owners began to sell off lots. The owner of Farm A sold a large parcel to a family member. Four lots were subdivided from Farm B, but they were located at the edge of the farm and didn't interfere with farming on the rest of the property.

4.8 A dramatic change took place in the 1970s. A 100-acre parcel in Farm A was subdivided into 16 lots served by a new road. A 53-acre lot sold to a family member in the 1950s was divided into three parcels. On Farm B two more lots were created, including a large field across from the farmhouse. Most of the farmland shifted to residential development.

4.9 In the 1980s, the remaining open land on Farm B was divided into 10 lots served by a new road, and the last large parcel on Farm A was split.

4.10 Farm C, which had been farmed through the 1980s, was sold in the early 1990s. The new owner began to sell off lots. Six large lots were created and were soon transformed into an enclave of estate homes for suburban families.

tourists to hike on their trails, stay in their bed and breakfasts, and buy local crafts and food products.

Within 40 years an agricultural area in Shelburne, Vermont **(Fig. 4.6)**, was transformed from three farms to 47 large house lots, ranging in size from two to 17 acres. What began with the sale of a few lots at the edge of a farm ended with the wholesale subdivision of the properties. After a few individual lot sales along the road frontage, property owners proposed larger subdivisions of 10 and 16 lots served by new roads. Over time, older lots were split again into smaller lots. This piecemeal approach to the development of these three farms resulted in the unnecessary fragmentation of a valuable natural resource (**Figs. 4.6 to 4.10**).

This agricultural area has been lost to development despite town plan policies that have supported the protection of farmland since the 1960s. The 1964 town plan issued a warning that "Shelburne's land use development is shifting from its previous agricultural base to one of mixed residential, commercial and industrial land development."[7] By 1974, the town was characterized as a "residential-agricultural community which has retained much of its rural quality while experiencing rapid growth and development."[8] Despite these development trends, the town held onto its goal to "preserve open space and to provide a sound economic basis for its maintenance as open space."[9] Again in 1980, the town insisted "agricultural land is of primary importance to the town," and cluster development was encouraged to "reduce the current trend of chopping up viable farmland."[10] Even in 1999 the town does not appear to have lost hope for sav-

ing farmland. The town still aims to "maintain the agricultural, economic, environmental and aesthetic benefits provided by Shelburne's rural lands" by such means as cluster development, lower densities in rural areas, and stricter subdivision and zoning standards.[11]

While the town wanted to preserve its rural, agricultural character, the piecemeal development of the three farms in the area is indicative of the town's inability to achieve this goal through regulation. The town's subdivision regulations didn't allow the town to look at each farm as a whole before it was broken up and to arrive at a plan that would permit some development to go forward while still keeping most of the agricultural resource intact. In addition, until 1979 the town exempted two lot subdivisions from any review. If the town had instead required an acceptable plan for the entire parcel before any lots were split off, a better solution might have been found.

LAND USE REGULATIONS

Market pressures can fuel the pattern of low-density subdivision of the countryside, but local land use regulations also have a significant role. As noted in *Incremental Change*, an unseen framework of development factors determines the fate of each parcel of land. Land use regulations (subdivision and zoning) are one important component of that framework. Subdivision regulations are the rules that guide the division of a parcel of land into lots. Zoning regulations establish the lot sizes and dimensions for each parcel and dictate what can be built on the land. The developer of each parcel follows the rules laid down in the town's zoning and subdivision regulations.

If the process of reviewing and approving development is piecemeal, fragmentation is inevitable. Under many subdivision regulations, parcels are reviewed in isolation, without an eye toward a total plan for the area. This leads to a disconnected and broken pattern. For example, the woods on one parcel of land may lose the connection with those on an adjoining parcel. The result is smaller patches of woods rather than one larger, connected forest.

Figure 4.11 illustrates the predicament towns find themselves in when their review process focuses on individual projects rather than a long-range plan. Shown here are three subdivisions in the Town of Williston, Vermont, that were reviewed as isolated projects. Each subdivision is a cluster development; in return for the protection of common open space, the developer was allowed smaller lots. Clustering enabled the town to protect drainageways, to secure pedestrian easements through each pro-

ject, and to achieve some of the goals of the town's open space plan. However, the resulting pattern of open spaces is fragmented—primarily serving separate rows of homes but not offering the residents any meaningful place for recreation, such as ball fields and hiking trails, or for simple enjoyment of a pastoral landscape. If the homes had been more compactly sited, one large area of surrounding open space could have been established.

Like many small towns within metropolitan areas, Williston has experienced rapid growth while its urban neighbors have leveled off in population. Many city residents, as well as newcomers to the area, have moved out to the edge, to towns like this. What was, in 1960, a farming community of 1,484 people became, by 1990, a suburb with three times the population. In the past decade the town has continued to grow faster than any other community in the county.

Williston was unprepared for the number of people that would descend on it. Like most small towns facing a major growth spurt, it had no idea what the community would look like after the build out was complete. In the late 1970s there was no plan in place to protect farmland or to steer new residential growth into the village. The town adopted zoning (1963) and subdivision regulations (1972) to handle the growth, but the regulations were deficient. Development occurred randomly, creating a pattern of fragmentation. By 1990 the town did adopt an open space plan but as further development unfolded, problems were still evident. Throughout the 1990s the town reexamined its plan and bylaws, trying to find a better

4.11 *Three cluster subdivisions with disconnected and fragmented open space in Williston, Vermont.*

way to grow and to avoid the mistakes of the past that have led to fragmented open space lands.

Zoning may also contribute to fragmentation by permitting incompatible development in areas of town also designated for natural resource protection. For example, when a community designates farmland as a commercial or industrial zone, it can hasten the decline of agriculture on that land. **Figures 4.12 to 4.15** show the shrinking of productive farmland outside one Vermont village. This level, well-drained land once held some of the town's best soils for farming. In 1941, the area shown was almost entirely occupied by farms. By 1963, some homes and a few businesses had popped up along the highway that leads out of the nearby downtown. More soon followed, appropriating the fields closest to the road. The practice of building on cropland outside of the village had been going on for several years, when, in 1972, the town chose to make it official through its new zoning regulations. It established a large zone (several times the size of the nearby downtown) for commercial and industrial businesses. Through this zoning decision, the town declined the opportunity to protect the soil for future generations by restricting this land to agricultural uses. Although farming was still allowed after 1972, there was an increased financial incentive to sell or build. By 1994, the farms had ceased to operate and the remaining fields were being held until the time was ripe for commercial development.[12]

If, in 1972, this land had been zoned for agricultural use, with only very limited residential uses permitted, instead of commercial uses, the pressure to subdivide would have been controlled and the larger fields could have been maintained. Developers would have looked elsewhere, like the existing downtown, for a place to build. If there was no room downtown, the community would have had a third choice that would have benefited both developers and farmers. It could have limited the commercial zone to a smaller area and designated the rest of the prime soil for agriculture. In a smaller zone with regulations that allow high density, developers would have had the reason and the means to use the space more efficiently, fitting more activity into a smaller area and leaving the rest for farming.

4.12 Farm fields outside Morrisville, Vermont, in 1941. Source: U.S. Department of Agriculture, Natural Resource Conservation Service.

4.13 Farming is still extensive in 1963 although some strip development appears.

4.14 By 1974, the fields have become isolated and smaller.

4.15 By 1994, only a few small parcels of farmland remain around an area dominated by low-density commercial and industrial development.

FOREST FRAGMENTATION AND WILDLIFE HABITAT

The folks who bought house lots in Robinson Springs, a housing subdivision in Stowe, Vermont (**Fig. 4.16**), were drawn to this land by stunning views of the surrounding mountains and a secluded setting. They recognized the natural beauty of the place and settled in, building houses, driveways, and ponds, installing lawns, and landscaping. But what they probably weren't aware of, as they built their homes, was the impact they would have on the native plant and animal communities of this hillside.

Like most subdivisions in remote areas, Robinson Springs affected its environment in two ways. It altered the physical structure of the place, and it intensified human use of the area. These two changes shifted the ecological balance away from a rarer type of habitat and toward another, more common one. What had been a home for wildlife, occasionally visited by humans, became a home for humans with a diminished capacity to support wildlife.

This land, which was used for farming in the 19th century, was abandoned to the forces of natural succession in the 20th. By the 1970s, a new-growth hardwood forest with a diverse plant and animal population had returned. This section of forest played a key role in supporting wildlife. Not only did its unbroken canopy of trees provide food and shelter for many species; it also served as a regional connection for migrating animals.

In order to make the land accessible and provide picturesque views, the developer had to cut trees. The clearings that were made for roads, driveways, and lawns dissected the forest, creating smaller, isolated islands of

4.16 *Fragmented forest canopy plus roads and house sites in Robinson Springs, Stowe, Vermont.*

woods. The result was less shady, protected interior space and more sunny, exposed edges. The "edge effect" alters a forest community, shifting the habitat to favor common species like rabbit or raccoon over more rare animals. When a canopy is disturbed, competitor plant and animal species that thrive in the sunnier spaces can replace existing species.[13] The long, circuitous road serving this development acts as a barrier to the native population of deep woods species and, at the same time, offers an opportunity for predator species to penetrate.

Forest canopies are often broken up by storms, fires, or logging operations. But unlike those disturbances, in which the trees grow back and the forest habitat eventually re-establishes itself, a housing development introduces a permanent human presence into a wilderness area. People, dogs, cars, lights, and noise scare off many animals, preventing them from using the woods for food and shelter.

Robinson Springs had an especially big impact on the black bear. Like fishers, moose, and bobcats, black bears depend on large blocks of dense forest to survive. They need stands of beech trees to provide nuts in the fall and wetland forests to supply green plants in the early spring. And they need to travel along forested corridors between the two locations.

As the forest canopy on this hillside became fragmented, bears, which favor the interior, were left without the cover they need. The smaller bits of woods left over after subdivision are not hospitable to them. There are fewer beech stands to provide them with food and, more importantly, the remaining beeches are now in an environment that bears cannot use.

And the construction of Robinson Springs had a larger effect on the bear population of the area. Before the houses were built, this land served as a corridor that reached a critical link across the highway in the valley below. Bears would move down this hillside, cross the road, and reach thousands of acres of forest on the other side. Once the woods were cut, the bears not only lost their local connection to feeding grounds but also their regional access to a broader habitat. Because the lots in this subdivision are large and the development covers a big area, it presents a substantial barrier to migrating bears.

Ecosystems that contain the many elements that can support black bears also offer the complex conditions to sustain a broad diversity of plants and animals. This is why wildlife biologists consider the black bear to be an "umbrella species." The presence of black bears in a landscape is an indicator of healthy biodiversity.[14]

What's so great about diversity? While scientists don't know exactly how many species are needed, they believe that biodiversity is necessary for a stable and resilient ecosystem. With a wider range of plants and animals present in a given forest, the whole system is more resistant to the effects of disease, fire, or other disruptions. Even if some species are disrupted, others will survive to maintain the forest. This is true for plants as well as animals. But as people move into uninhabited regions, where native plant communities are dominant, they introduce exotic plants that can threaten the plant diversity of the existing forest. As earth is moved to create building lots, the soil is exposed, providing an opening for exotic seeds. Seeds can be imported by the wind, by birds, on the bucket of a backhoe, or in a bale of hay. Homeowners introduce invaders unknowingly as they landscape their yards. Each trip to the garden store has the potential to introduce a competitor to the surrounding ecosystem. Plants such as yellow flag iris, burning bush, japanese barberry, and norway maples, widely popular for their landscape qualities, can quickly spread to the surrounding woodlands or wetlands and crowd out less aggressive native species.[15]

In Maine, a state task force investigating the effects of sprawl development on wildlife defined the relationship between habitat fragmentation and decreasing diversity in a series of diagrams (**Fig. 4.17**). These illustrations depict different points on a development continuum. In the column below each diagram is a list of species that the land can sustain. Tier 1 represents undeveloped land. Tier 2 shows the same landscape fragmented into 500–2,500-acre blocks of forest. As the land becomes divided into smaller and smaller parcels of undisturbed land, the list shrinks to fewer and fewer species. In the haphazard and incremental process of development, as suburbia emerges, new roads and house lots eventually squeeze out the hawk and the mink, favoring urban survivors like the skunk and the squirrel.

The lists are not absolute. Depending on the context, some animals can survive in smaller blocks of open space. Species that require larger blocks of open space will sometimes enter a more developed area and will become habituated to it, if they can move freely between it and a larger

tract of forest. The key is to preserve the corridors through which wildlife migrates. If left undisturbed, ridgelines, wetlands, and other riparian corridors that connect habitats can extend the range of many species, offering them a chance for survival in a landscape that has been compromised by development.[16]

Whether building homes or businesses, Americans usually seek out the countryside, where land is cheap and there's plenty of elbow room. We might choose a site because it is close to an interstate exit or because it has a lovely view. But what we really seem to be after is the luxury of feeling that space is unlimited, that we'll never have to worry about how to park the cars or turn the trucks, how wide the aisles can be or how big the bathrooms are. When it seems that there is plenty of space, we tend to squander it. Why build two stories when there is room for one story at twice the size? Why put the house on the edge of the field when the whole 10 acres is one big building site?

As we spread out and the impact of sprawl becomes clear, it appears that there is, in fact, a bigger price tag for all the space. The cost is paid by the working landscape, by outdoor recreation, and by wildlife. If we want to stop trading away these public assets, we need to rethink our attitudes toward space and how we use it.

Tier 1 *Undeveloped*	Tier 3 *500-2500 acre blocks*	Tier 3 *100-500 acre blocks*	Tier 4 *20-100 acre blocks*	Tier 5 *1-20 acre blocks*

Tier 1	Tier 3	Tier 3	Tier 4	Tier 5
raccoon	raccoon	raccoon	raccoon	raccoon
hare	hare	hare	hare	
coyote				
small rodent	small rodent	small rodent	small rodent	small rodent
porcupine	porcupine	porcupine	porcupine	
bobcat				
cottontail	cottontail	cottontail	cottontail	cottontail
beaver	beaver	beaver	beaver	
black bear				
squirrel	squirrel	squirrel	squirrel	squirrel
weasel	weasel	weasel	weasel	
mink	mink	mink		
fisher				
woodchuck	woodchuck	woodchuck	woodchuck	
deer	deer	deer		
muskrat	muskrat	muskrat	muskrat	muskrat
moose	moose			
red fox	red fox	red fox	red fox	red fox
songbirds	songbirds	songbirds	songbirds	songbirds
sharp-shinned hawk	sharp-shinned hawk	sharp-shinned hawk		
bald eagle	bald eagle			
skunk	skunk	skunk	skunk	skunk
cooper's hawk	cooper's hawk	cooper's hawk		
harrier	harrier	harrier		
broad-winged hawk	broad-winged hawk	broad-winged hawk		
goshawk	goshawk			
kestrel	kestrel	kestrel		
red-tailed hawk	red-tailed hawk			
horned owl	horned owl	horned owl		
raven	raven			
barred owl	barred owl	barred owl		
osprey	osprey	osprey		
turkey vulture	turkey vulture	turkey vulture		
turkey	turkey	turkey		
reptiles	reptiles	reptiles	most reptiles	most reptiles
garter snake	garter snake	garter snake	garter snake	
ring-neck snake	ring-neck snake	ring-neck snake	ring-neck snake	
amphibians	amphibians	most amphibians	most amphibians	most amphibians
wood frog	wood frog	wood frog		

4.17

EARLY TOWN BUILDING

To understand a different approach, it's helpful to get into the mindset of earlier town builders. Brandon, Vermont (**Fig. 4.18**), is a model of compactness. It sits in the midst of a rural area, with open fields and woods all around. A century ago, as it was growing, the idea of locating these houses and businesses on large lots in those fields was unthinkable. They used the space available to them carefully, allocating every square foot to a useful purpose, whether it was for public space or private building.

Brandon is not as dense as it could be. There is more space between buildings here than there would be in a city. There are more lawns and even some woods. But it is far denser than contemporary settlements, and unlike those in contemporary developments, the green spaces between the buildings in Brandon are more than just leftover scraps. If you take the village as it looks today and pick it apart, you can see the difference. **Figures 4.19 to 4.22** (page 84), show a sequence—like putting together a jigsaw puzzle—that reveals how usable space interlocks, leaving no fragments. The first shows the streets, civic buildings and public spaces of the village. The second shows the businesses of the village, which, like the public spaces, are tightly connected to the streets. When the neighborhoods are added, they, too, are contiguous with the other built-up areas. With all the built elements placed back in the picture, five large chunks of open land are left (**Fig. 4.21**, page 84). Compare this with the highway interchange shown at the beginning of the chapter (**Fig. 4.22**, page 84) and you can see how a thrifty use of space can prevent the fragmentation of open land.

How can today's communities stop the spread of low-density development to precious resource lands? First, by channeling growth into the town's center in a compact pattern, like that of Brandon. Second, by actively protecting those farm fields, wetlands, shorelines, and forests through a combination of regulation and land conservation.

4.18 Brandon Village in Brandon, Vermont, 1996.

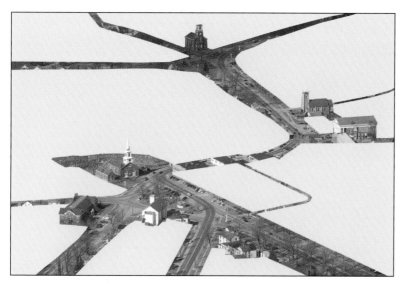

4.19 Streets, civic buildings and public spaces added.

4.20 Businesses added.

4.21 Neighborhoods added, open space remaining.

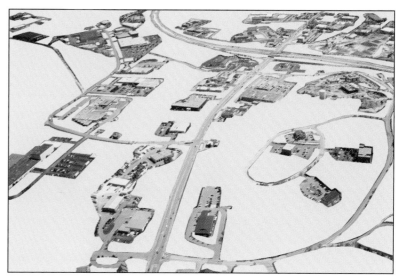

4.22 Buildings, parking lots, and roads at the interchange shown earlier (Fig. 4.2).

A VISION FOR PROTECTING FARMLAND AND WILDLIFE HABITAT

Citizens in Charlotte, Vermont, concerned about the fragmentation of farmland and wildlife habitat in their suburbanizing community, decided to get involved when it was time to rewrite the town plan. They joined other residents in a series of workshops to develop a vision for the future of the town. There was agreement that, in the face of dramatic change, the town needed to retain and enhance its most significant values: the quality of the rural landscape and environment, the diversity of its population, the small town character, historic features, high- quality services, and strong participation by residents in government.[17]

With the vision as a guide, the residents then formed eight committees, including one on farming and another on natural resources. The farming committee met with farmers, inventoried all the farmland in the town, and recommended the establishment of four agricultural management districts, each with its own set of guidelines. Their recommendations were incorporated into the town plan.

Aided by topographic maps, members of the natural resources committee set out to interview local residents who harvest, study, or protect the town's animals, fish, and birds. They then mapped the town's wildlife habitat areas and compared their maps to aerial photographs. Their work was field checked by wildlife biologists and incorporated into a map of "locally significant" wildlife habitat areas that was then included in the town plan.

The residents didn't stop there. They knew that having a good town plan was only a first step. After the town plan was adopted, zoning and subdivision regulations were rewritten to bring them into conformance with the town plan. Now, town subdivision regulations require all buildings, lots, roadways, sewage disposal sites and sewer and water lines to be located so as to retain productive farmland in the agricultural management districts as part of "protected open space." The standards require that the guidelines for each of the four management districts be followed and mandate buffers between homes and farm operations. The regulations also protect locally significant wildlife habitat.

An example of how these provisions work in Charlotte is illustrated in **Fig. 4.23** (page 86). This 420-acre farm was proposed for subdivision in several different phases. In the first subdivision, town planners required the houses to be clustered in a wooded area along a rural dirt road to protect the broad, open fields. Although the open fields were part of the house lots, the owners were not permitted to fence the fields and were required to lease the fields back to a farmer. In the next phase of the subdivision, house lots were set back off the road in some woods at the rear of the property. The open fields along the road were set aside in a separate parcel and were protected by an easement granted to the Vermont Land Trust. In the final phase an additional 120 acres were protected through the land trust. When the subdivision was complete, a total of 26 house lots were created and 310 acres, or 74 percent of the farm, were protected through conservation easements and no-build zones. Today, two farmers use the conserved land to grow hay and corn.

There was still more work to do. People in this town knew that plans

4.23 *After taking steps to protect its farmland, the town of Charlotte preserved 310 acres of this 420-acre farm for permanent agricultural use. Townwide, some 4,000 acres are protected for agriculture, most of it in large contiguous blocks.*

and regulations weren't the only answer to protecting land, so they voted to establish a town conservation fund by adding two cents to the tax rate. The fund has been used to leverage state and private dollars for the preservation of farmland, establish a new town park, and protect a locally significant wildlife corridor along a river. Over 4,000 acres of farmland and conservation land have been protected in the town as a result of its vision, regulations and the conservation fund.

KEEPING THE COUNTRY PRODUCTIVE

In the town of Swanton, Vermont, farmers have been working with land conservation organizations and the state of Vermont on measures to protect their land, with dramatic results. Over 5,000 acres have been conserved through the acquisition of development rights on farmland. On each of the protected farms (**Fig. 4.24**, page 88), the owners have sold their development rights for a value established by an appraisal. Money to buy the development rights comes from the Vermont Housing and Conservation Board or a private foundation through grants to the Vermont Land Trust or the state Department of Agriculture, Food, and Markets.

Many states and some regions have established similar farmland protection programs that pay farmers for their development rights. Although development rights are removed from the land, the farmer continues to own and farm the land. The value of the land is reduced by removal of the development rights, thus lowering the property taxes on the land and often lowering the purchase price of the farm when it is sold. These programs have been successful in maintaining agricultural land and a rural way of life in many parts of the country.

Swanton's excellent climate and good soils have made it a center for dairy farming, yet, because of its prime location on the shores of Lake Champlain, it is not immune to development. Due to the challenges of dairying, farmers are often tempted by offers to purchase lots. The easement program offers farmers an alternative to selling off valuable agricultural land. The Vermont Land Trust negotiates the terms of the sale with each farmer and makes provisions, where necessary, for farm labor hous-

4.24 In Swanton, Vermont, farmers have sold development rights to more than 5,000 acres of land ("protected") outside the village center ("village"), creating a large, unbroken block of permanently protected farmland. Other farms in the area have requested protection for their land as well ("in progress").

KEEPING THE COUNTRY WILD

ing and family lots. Although farmers and town officials were skeptical about the program at first, they now fully embrace it, and there is more demand for funds than the state can provide.

The easement program has strengthened the Swanton farm economy. Farmers have used the funds to buy more land, pay off debt, make capital improvements, or to sell their farms at an affordable price to a son or daughter. "The easement program has made people stay in farming," said Lynn Fresn, a farmer who has sold her development rights.[18] It has also helped local farm-dependent businesses, such as veterinarians, equipment dealers, hardware stores, grain and seed suppliers, and fertilizer companies.

The easement program is vitally important to the achievement of Swanton's town plan goal to "maintain and support a viable agricultural economy including farming, forestry and other related activities." The large block of protected land surrounds the southern end of the village of Swanton and helps reinforce another town plan goal to "be a traditional New England settlement surrounded by open agricultural lands."

While farmers were taking action to protect the future productivity of the land in Swanton, people in Stowe, Vermont, were working to keep a corner of their town wild. As homes appeared high on the hillside of Robinson Springs (shown earlier in this chapter), Stowe residents wondered whether the land on the other side of the mountain would meet the same fate. It had become clear that there was a market for high-elevation house lots. Robinson Springs proved that despite the high costs, homeowners had the resources and the desire to extend roads and utilities into remote land.

As they lost their habitat at Robinson Springs, black bears in the area could fall back on the large tracts of unspoiled forest in the neighboring hills. One high valley, known locally as Sterling Forest, is home to species like bear, moose, and coyote, all of which depend on large tracts of heavy forest (**Fig. 4.25**, page 90). It is contiguous with an extensive state forest covering the highest peak in Vermont and has many of the same conditions that Robinson Springs once had, including the mix of trees and plants that rarer species depend on for survival.[19]

In the 1970s, when Robinson Springs was subdivided, the impacts of development on wildlife habitat and migration were not seriously considered or even clearly understood. In the public record of permit hearings for this development, there is no discussion of how road cuts and house clearings would limit the range and food supply of black bears, or how their fear of humans would prevent bears from reaching the forest further down the hill. But by the early 1990s, when 2,150 acres of land came up for sale in Sterling Forest, Stowe's planners understood exactly what was at

4.25 *This high valley, known locally as Sterling Forest, is home to species like bear, moose, and coyote that depend on large tracts of heavy forest. It has many of the same conditions to support wildlife that Robinson Springs once had, including the mix of trees and plants that rarer species depend on for survival.*

risk. And it wasn't just wildlife habitat, but water quality, outdoor recreation, and the wild and scenic character of a high-elevation environment.

They began a local conservation effort, called the Tricentennial Project, to protect the entire upper watershed of Sterling Brook as well as other key parcels in town: a working dairy farm and a scenic hill farm. Stowe was about to celebrate its 200th anniversary, and community leaders hoped, as residents looked back on their history, that they would think about the next 100 years as well. In a classic example of a public-private partnership, they succeeded in raising $1 million to protect the entire 2,150 acres. About $300,000 was offered up by the taxpayers of Stowe, who voted by a margin of 60 percent to fund the project through a larger bond. The balance was given by the state's conservation board, a private foundation, and adjoining landowners (**Fig. 4.26**).[20]

4.26 *Some 2,150 acres of land will remained undeveloped in Sterling Forest.*

TAMING RESORT DEVELOPMENT

Residents of tiny Peru, Vermont, also decided that they didn't want to see the town's rural character destroyed by piecemeal development. Faced in the 1980s with the expansion of a major ski area, the town feared that seasonal home development would break up the remaining open fields and extensive woodlands bordering the Green Mountain National Forest. Local leaders decided to rewrite the town plan and zoning regulations to address these concerns. The new documents changed the way the town thought about development. Now there are rules in place to protect the historic village, to preserve the scenic beauty of a major highway, and to require lower densitites and cluster development on rural agricultural and forest land.

The town views its village as the heart of the community and its commercial and administrative center. It encourages mixed uses, small-scale buildings, and commercial establishments that cater first to the needs of residents and secondarily to the needs of tourists. The town limits the size of commercial uses to 8,000 square feet and prohibits fast food and drive-through restaurants and banks. A townscape preservation board administers standards for preservation of historic landmarks and compatible new construction.

Along a scenic state highway corridor, the town limits driveway access; preserves scenic vistas, views, and meadowlands; and sets commercial and industrial buildings 200 feet back from the edge of the right of way. Density bonuses are offered for developments that dedicate conservation easements for scenic views or vistas and that improve traffic conditions along the highway. Existing vegetation that screens buildings along the road must be kept.

In the rural areas of the town, landowners may subdivide three lots before they are required to go through a cluster development review process for any further subdivision. Under the cluster rules, lands with severe limitations for development cannot be counted for determining how many homes may be built on the parcel. Building sites and roads must be located away from agricultural and scenic areas, and special measures must be taken around deeryards.

The restrictions on development in the rural areas and along the scenic highway also help to support development where the town would like to see it: in its village and in existing built-up areas.

4.27 Some of the 1,700 acres of land and 12 miles of lakes and river shoreline protected by the Winooski Valley Park District.

TAKING A REGIONAL APPROACH

In the 1960s and 1970s growth pressures around Burlington, Vermont, raised alarms about the loss of open space and public access to traditional fishing, swimming, and hiking areas. Several towns banded together in 1972 to found the Winooski Valley Park District in order to "acquire and manage open space, wildlife habitat, farmland and natural areas, and to help plan for the protection of the lands and waters of the Winooski River watershed." Today seven communities work together on this regional approach to saving open space.

As a result of the towns' efforts, a swath of green is now protected along the Winooski River in the City of Burlington (**Fig. 4.27**). Within this preserved area are acres of prime agricultural land still managed by area farmers, the historic home of one of Vermont's most famous rebels (Ethan Allen), wetlands and natural areas, bike paths, and gardens. These lands offer residents in nearby urban centers an oasis of green in the summer months and a quiet place to snowshoe or cross-country ski in the winter.

Nearly 30 years after it began the park district owns over 1,700 acres of land and 12 miles of lake and river shoreland along the Winooski River and within the surrounding watershed. Over $2.5 million from the towns, government grants, private donations, and memberships have been spent on acquisitions and improvements. Most of the purchases have been made in response to development pressures that threatened important regional resources. Today, the interconnected properties give people the assurance that beyond their neighborhoods is a continuous edge of land that will be conserved forever.

NOTES

1. Herbert Ladd Towle. "The Every-day Automobile," *Harper's Weekly,* Vol. LV, No. 2824, February 4, 1911, p. 11.

2. Kenneth Johnson and Calvin L. Beale. "The Rural Rebound Revisited," *American Demographics,* July 1995.

3. Sierra Business Council. *Planning for Prosperity: Building Successful Communities in the Sierra Nevada,* 1997, p. 7.

4. Maine State Planning Office, *Markets for Traditional Neighborhoods,* August 1999, p. 5.

5. David Olinger. "We Caused Sprawl Ourselves," Denver Post Online, February 7, 1999.

6. American Farmland Trust, "Farming on the Edge," 1997.

7. Shelburne, Vermont. *Town Plan, Shelburne, Vermont,* 1964, p. 4.

8. Shelburne, Vermont. *Town Plan, Shelburne, Vermont,* 1974, p. 7.

9. *Ibid.,* p. 1.

10. Shelburne, Vermont. *Town Plan, Shelburne, Vermont,* 1980, p. 64.

11. Shelburne, Vermont. *Comprehensive Plan, Vol. II, Goals, Objectives and Strategies, Shelburne, Vermont,* April 13, 1999, pp. 9-10.

12. Data source: U.S. Soil Conservation Service aerial photographs, 1941, 1963, 1972, and 1994.

13. For a more detailed description of biodiversity and the edge effect, see Malcolm L. Hunter, *Wildlife, Forests, and Forestry: Principles of Managing Forests for Biological Diversity,* Prentice Hall, 1990.

14. Conversation with John Austin, District Wildlife Biologist, Vermont Fish and Wildlife Department, September 1999.

15. Leslie J. Mehrhoff, "The Biology of Plant Invasions," *New England Wildflower,* Vol. 2, No. 3, pp. 8-10.

16. "Designing Communities to Protect Wildlife Habitat and Accommodate Development," Report of the Patterns of Development Task Force, Maine Environmental Priorities Project, July 1997.

17. Charlotte, Vermont. *Charlotte Town Plan,* 1990, p. 1.

18. Vermont Housing and Conservation Board. Annual Report to the General Assembly, 1997, p. 22.

19. "Watson Forest: Natural Features Inventory and Management Recommendations." Report prepared for the Stowe Conservation Commission by Black Bear Consultants, May 1996.

20. Conversation with Brian Shupe, former director of planning and zoning, Stowe, Vermont, July 2000.

DIVIDE AND DRIVE

As growth began to spread out from the City of St. Albans in the 1960s, the surrounding Town of St. Albans decided it would manage future development by establishing zoning regulations.   According to these rules, homes were to be placed in a distinct residential zone separated from other uses. Businesses, retail stores, restaurants, and offices were relegated to a commercial zone, and industry (manufacturing and warehousing) to an industrial zone. Over the years the town has evolved according to this arrangement. Each of these uses—residential, commercial, and industrial—has developed within the space allocated to it (**Fig. 5.2**). However, as a result of its planning the town has lost something that the neighboring City of St. Albans has retained. In the city, tightly knit neighborhoods enable residents to walk to shops, city hall, church, and the town green. Workers in businesses down by the old railroad yards can walk downtown for lunch or errands. In the town, residents and workers must drive for even the most basic need.

St. Albans Town, like many small towns, wanted to provide its residents with space and privacy at a good distance from the noise and traffic of commerce and the dangers of pollution. Most communities thought they were doing a good thing by seeking an alternative to the older settlement pattern of homes above stores, stores next to industries, and schools next to homes. Planners and government officials encouraged this strategy. As early as the 1940s, a publication of the Federal Housing Administration encouraged the separation of uses. "Undesirable or inappropriate uses of land such as business and industrial uses invading residential areas; detri-

mental mixtures of apartments and detached dwellings; turning of major traffic thoroughfares through subdivisions; and similar conditions quickly break down neighborhood character and impair real estate values."[1]

Instead of protecting community character and quality of life, the separation of uses and activities has spread too far (**Fig. 5.3**). People drive to work, to day care, to pick up groceries and dry cleaning, and to take their children to soccer practice or music lessons. It is not surprising that the average number of daily trips each person takes is rising.[2] Between 1980 and 1995, the total vehicles miles traveled in the U.S. increased by nearly 60 percent while population increased by only 16 percent.[3] Frustrated by the time they are spending in their cars, people clamor for better roads that will connect them to their various destinations faster.

There are other consequences to separating land uses. People who don't drive are finding themselves increasingly isolated from jobs, shops, and services. Some employers are seeing the costs of doing business rise while productivity declines as workers spend endless hours behind the wheel. Residents of urban and village centers find that they can no longer buy groceries, hardware, and clothing in their downtowns and must drive miles to new commercial shopping centers to obtain necessities. With the improvements to telecommunications and e-commerce, more individuals can work anywhere they want and as a result, they often choose remote locations. Yet, some of these people are feeling disconnected from their communities and their friends.

To overcome isolation, lack of access to basic goods and services, and

5.2 *Zoning in St. Albans Town separates different uses into distinct areas. (Simulated image.)*

5.3 *Growth in St. Albans Town proceeds according to residential, commercial, and industrial districts.*

road rage, many people now want to live near work, be part of a neighborhood, have their children walk to school, and get supplies nearby. Some employers are pitching in to help build housing near their plants, and retailers are studying the market potential of downtowns. No longer content with the old approaches to separating uses, communities are taking another look at their zoning codes to see how they can encourage more mixed uses and diverse housing projects.

How did land uses get separated? In early settlements, many different activities took place within one building. Townspeople gathered for meetings in private homes, which also offered lodging for travelers. As communities grew, taverns were built and people congregated not only to eat and drink but also to discuss town politics. With time, the community outgrew these spaces and constructed special purpose buildings, such as meeting houses and churches. Eventually, stores were built as well. Thus, what once could be accommodated within one building gradually shifted to multiple buildings, each with its own separate purpose but all within close proximity.

As communities grew and town centers and cities emerged, the number and size of uses multiplied. Yet they stayed within a relatively compact area. When the growth exceeded the capacity of the center to handle it, new centers sometimes cropped up nearby or adjacent farmland was converted to home sites. Nevertheless, these places retained a mixed use, compact pattern. In some rural areas, the center may have consisted of a few homes, a church, a meeting hall, and a general store. In larger communities, there were apartments, single-family homes, boarding houses, numerous stores, several churches, industries, schools, meeting halls, and libraries. All these different uses and activities were easily accessible to all by foot.

St. Johnsbury, Vermont (**Fig. 5.4**), exemplifies this pattern. In this village we see a mixture of uses that reinforces a civic center and creates a symbol of pride. Businesses and homes are not awkwardly placed in their own separate pods but integrated through street networks and building design and layout. Apartments are located over stores in handsome downtown buildings. Other homes are set along sidewalks, enabling residents to walk the short distance to the commercial area. Government offices and a museum are located in historic public buildings.

By contrast, in a growing area of Manchester, Vermont (**Fig. 5.5**), residential developments have sprung up on fields outside the center of town. Businesses have moved onto open land that is close by but disconnected from nearby homes. This contemporary settlement pattern reflects homeowners' desires for green space and privacy and businesses' desire for convenient parking.

5.4 Stores, churches, public buildings, single-family houses, and apartment buildings are close together in St. Johnsbury, Vermont.

5.5 Stores, homes, and businesses spread out into separate enclaves away from the historic town center of Manchester, Vermont.

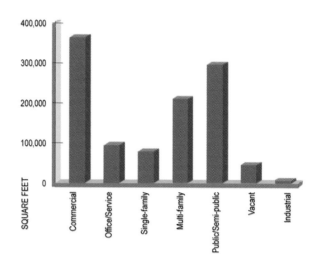

5.6 and 5.7 (right) A 44-acre downtown provides space for over 1.7 million square feet of housing, commerce, and industrial and civic uses.

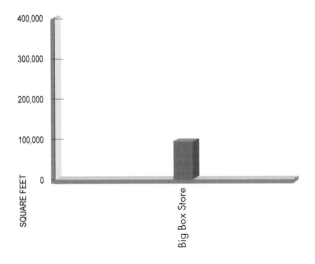

5.8 and 5.9 (right) A 44-acre site in a cornfield near an interstate interchange provides space for one big box store measuring 100,000 square feet.

DIVERSITY IN DOWNTOWNS, MONOTONY IN FIELDS

The historic diversity of downtowns and the contemporary homogeneity of newly developed areas can be vividly illustrated by a comparison of two 44-acre sites, one in downtown St. Albans City and one in a farm field near an interstate interchange in St. Albans Town (**Figs. 5.6,** page 100 and **5.8**, page 101). The downtown contains more than 1.7 million square feet, with many different uses plus streets, sidewalks, and a town green. The only development proposed on the same size piece of land in the field was a 100,000-square-foot big box store and its parking and loading areas, access drives, and landscaping.

St. Alban City's downtown is diverse, reflecting its evolution over 150 years as the government, commercial, industrial, and residential center of the surrounding region. Within its 44 acres one finds offices, retail stores, services, single-family homes, apartments, public buildings, industrial uses, parks, streets, sidewalks, and parking (**Fig. 5.7**, page 100). A network of intersecting streets lined with sidewalks makes all of downtown highly accessible on foot or by car. The mixture of public buildings—city hall, post office, library, and nearby school—creates a civic presence and keeps people in touch with community events, activities, and issues.

The only use proposed for the 44-acre big box site was commercial (**Fig 5.9**, page 101). Local zoning prohibited homes and public buildings there. People could only get there by car, and once there all they could do was shop.

Believing that the giant store would draw sales from downtown and village businesses, lower property values, undercut jobs, require more public reinvestment in the downtown, and increase demands on services, the State Environmental Board denied a permit for the project.[5] The board's decision was upheld by the Vermont Supreme Court.[6] If the project had occurred in the downtown (where space was found for an 80,500-square-foot, two-story store), many of these adverse impacts would have been avoided and residents and employees would have been able to get to the store on foot or by car.

PUBLIC POLICY FUELS SEPARATION

The incremental development of the Route 7 highway corridor in South Burlington, Vermont (also featured in "Introduction"), provides an example of public policy leading, parcel by parcel, to a single-purpose commercial strip (**Fig. 5.10**, page 104). Very early in the development of Route 7, South Burlington lost an opportunity to follow the lead of planners of early New England villages by creating a new, compact, mixed-use center to meet the needs of a growing residential area.

As early as the 1940s, local officials promoted commercial activity along Route 7 by rezoning small areas for business. Hoping to cash in on the highway's strategic advantages, developers and business owners came to the town hall to request zone changes for their new enterprises. The town willingly sanctioned their individual proposals until, in the 1960s, the decision was made to zone the entire strip 300 feet back on either side exclusively for business use.

This pattern was contrary to the advice of the Federal Housing Administration, which in the 1940s promoted compact commercial areas that served local neighborhoods. The federal agency encouraged commercial buildings to "be designed together as a group and not as a series of unrelated separate stores."[7] Just off Route 7 are residential subdivisions built between the 1930s and the 1950s. They feature small lots, narrow streets, and a pedestrian scale. By contrast, the commerce that followed them spread out along the length of the corridor instead of locating within a compact, central area easily accessible to the neighborhoods.

Although subdivisions and condominiums were built near Route 7 from the 1960s to the present, in many cases their streets did not intersect with the highway, thus preventing commuters from taking short cuts through residential neighborhoods. Most of the residential streets that did intersect the highway ended in cul-de-sacs, forcing homeowners out onto Route 7 for every trip (**Fig. 5.11**, page 105).

From the 1930s to the present, public policy failed to integrate residential uses and commercial activity along the Route 7 corridor. Through lack of foresight, or hindsight, local officials took the path of least resistance and bent to market pressures to allow the development of a commercial strip, serving residents from throughout the region. In nearby residential areas, homeowners cannot enjoy their own neighborhood commercial center. They must enter a stream of congested traffic to run even the simplest errand. Other residents are cut off from the highway by dead end streets. For their errands, they must take a roundabout route along secondary roads and eventually join the other drivers slowly making their way through the stoplights and traffic jams.

By creating a large-scale commercial strip along a major highway, public policy makers, developers, and business people in South Burlington were able to cater to a market much larger than local residents. As Route 7 filled up with commercial activity, the nearby downtown of Burlington, historically the regional center, began to lose its diversity. Car dealers, confined to small showrooms on Main Street, preferred the vast open spaces of the highway strip on which to display endless rows of cars. Furniture stores, department stores, auto supply stores, and grocery stores followed the route out of the central business district onto the strip, leaving the city with a narrower range of goods and services. Today the downtown has no furniture store, no hardware store, no auto dealership, only one department store, and no grocery store.[8] By losing its diversity, the downtown is no longer the county's dominant regional commercial center. Area residents shop the Route 7 corridor for cars and groceries, highway interchanges for shopping malls and big box stores, and the downtown for specialty items. The spread of regional commercial activities into so many distinct areas not only requires more driving but also makes it more difficult to introduce competing, but small, neighborhood activity centers that can serve the daily needs of residents.

Public subsidies are often targeted to single-use projects, such as industrial campuses and office parks, which encourage the separation of housing, commerce, and industry. In the Town of Milton, Vermont, a dramatic influx of state and federal dollars helped the development of an isolated industrial campus on 680 acres of open land (**Fig. 5.12**, page 106). The prospect of 2,500 new jobs in a community of 9,000 was a big selling point for the state and the town. State and federal agencies supported the employment center through utility subsidies and tax credit. The state issued over $10 million in tax credits to facilitate development. The town's sewer system, whose capacity was quadrupled as a result of the project, was aided by a federal grant and a state revolving fund loan. The town is paying back the state loan by means of increased school property taxes received from new town development, estimated to be $6.8 million. These

5.10 The Route 7 corridor in South Burlington, Vermont, in 1995.

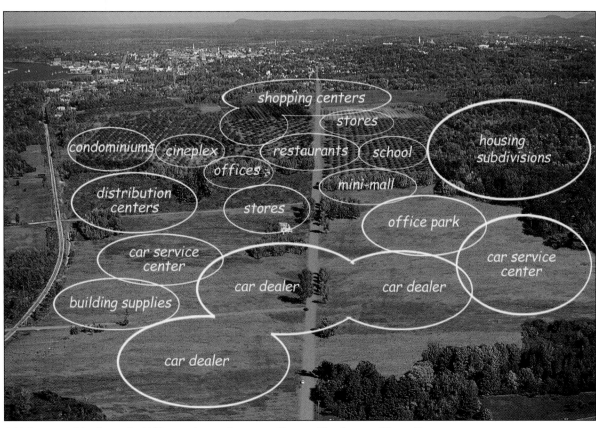

5.11 *Segregated land uses in 1995 superimposed on an earlier rural landscape of Route 7.*

5.12 State and federal funds helped the development of this isolated industrial campus on 680 acres of open land in Milton, Vermont.

5.13 Residents in Norwich, Vermont, worked to keep their post office in town.

5.14 The post office in Hinesburg, Vermont, was moved from the village to an open field at the edge.

tax revenues would otherwise have contributed to a statewide education fund. Now other Vermont taxpayers will have to make up for these lost revenues.

The single-purpose economic development subsidies did not address other community needs that could arise from the new industrial campus. There is no public transportation to the site, no shops and services within walking distance, and little nearby housing for workers. Most employees must drive to work, some from great distances. Some people who live far from the site cannot apply for jobs because they do not drive.[9] If these impacts had been considered up front, several changes could have been made. The new industry could have located in an established area where housing and services were available or jobs were needed. Alternatively, multi-purpose state subsidies—for economic development, housing, and transportation—could have helped pay for a new mixed center connected to the industrial campus.

Federal, state, and local governments also can influence the mixture of uses and housing types in local communities when they invest in public buildings. Local governments that build schools, town halls, or libraries on the edges of town centers disperse community activities, reduce the civic presence in the centers, and lower the opportunities for social interaction in a central place. State buildings that are moved to highway interchanges become inaccessible to the people living and working in nearby downtowns.

The U.S. Postal Service has an impact on every town in the nation. If it decides to build a new post office in a farm field outside the center of town, diversity and social interactions can suffer.

People in rural towns often go to the post office at least once a week. If the post office is located in the town center, people may also stop at the library, coffee shop, gas station, or the store. In any one of these places they are likely to run into their friends, neighbors, or town officials. Conversations may range from current community issues to arranging a get-together or dealing with a neighbor in need. However, if the post office is moved outside of the center to an isolated place, people must use their cars to get there, and will be less likely to run into other members of the community (**Figs. 5.13 and 5.14**).

5.15 A corporate campus in South Burlington sits alone, surrounded by open space.

REAL ESTATE MARKETS

Located in a field near the interstate highway in South Burlington is a landscaped corporate campus, distant from residential neighborhoods and town centers (**Fig. 5.15**). The large parking lots accommodate the automobiles that most employees must drive to get here. At lunch time, there will be no walks downtown for errands or home-cooked meals. The very isolation of the plant encourages workers to hang out at the plant during breaks.

Corporations have been looking for rural and suburban sites since the 1930s. These relatively undeveloped areas meet business needs for accessibility, flexibility, and security. Easy connections to the major roads offer advantages for the movement of goods and for employees who own cars. The sites offer space for flexible designs and room for expansion. There is enough land to display a corporate image through an eye-catching building in a landscaped setting.

Many businesses lack information on the long-term social and economic costs of spread-out, isolated, and single-use development.[10] The short term benefits of lower land costs and a relatively prompt and predictable permit process in small towns are often more important. The longer term problems of lack of accessibility for potential employees, higher infrastructure costs, and longer commuting times are less visible. As open space disappears and traffic congestion grows in sprawl locations, workers become harder to attract and retain.[11] Long commutes to an isolated work environment with limited or no shops, services, restaurants, or recreation facilities

is hardly appealing, but these factors are rarely considered in the first venture to a new location. However, the costs will emerge with time. Some companies try to remedy these problems with on-site cafeterias, lounges, recreation facilities, and, occasionally, day care. These additions, while helpful, do not make up for the distance from homes, friends, and community centers.

Businesses are not the only land use that have become isolated from other activities. Increasingly, new single-family homes are being located closer to open space and further from multi-family housing, commercial, and institutional development.[12] When asked about these trends, home builders say that these locations are what the "market" wants. Over 88 percent of a sample surveyed by the National Home Builders Association said that they preferred single-family detached homes, and 54 percent said that they would oppose townhouses in their neighborhood. Even more said that they would oppose multi-family housing.[13] It is not surprising that many new residential areas reflect the homogeneity espoused by "the market."

The subdivision in **Fig. 5.16** (page 110) reflects some homeowners' desire to live in a homogeneous neighborhood. The rows of cookie cutter homes suggest stability to residents. Duplexes, garage apartments, and apartment buildings do not intrude here.

The proliferation of single-family detached units has narrowed the range of housing choices in outlying areas and left less diversity in existing built-up neighborhoods. As more affluent and well-educated residents

5.16 *Repetitive rows of housing reflect a pattern of neighborhood homogeneity.*

locate in suburban areas and low-income and elderly households become isolated in older centers, the gap in income grows between families in suburban communities and those in urban areas. In Vermont, a sizable majority of the state's population and job growth has been in suburban towns, yet 76 percent of the new affordable housing units have been provided in traditional urban and village centers.[14] When residential neighborhoods lose their middle- and upper income base, single-family homes are often divided up into apartments by absentee landlords, and sales in nearby shops decline. With time, buildings deteriorate and stores close their doors.

MORE SEPARATION, MORE TRIPS

The isolation of homes, jobs, stores, and community buildings from one another fosters continued dependence on the automobile. The plight of "high mileage moms"—mothers who average more than an hour, more than five trips, and 29 miles in their cars each day—has been recently publicized.[15] The demands on these women increase especially where there are no transportation options for their children and elderly parents. However, it is not just the moms who are affected. Between 1969 and 1990, the length of the average work trip in the U.S. increased 17 percent and the average annual number of shopping trips per household grew 62 percent.[16] As more people move to their five acres in the countryside, more stores open in peripheral areas, and more employers vie for corporate estates, there will be longer trips, less opportunity for carpooling, and fewer trips by bicycle, foot, or transit (**Fig. 5.17**, page 112).

Not only are people spending more time in their cars, but they are also driving alone more often. Increased time alone in cars means less time for families, recreation, and civic activities. According to one source, "each additional 10 minutes in daily commuting time cuts involvement in community affairs by 10 percent" and has a strong adverse effect on informal social interaction.[17] Rural towns have certainly seen this effect. As more and more residents commute to other towns for work and shopping, fewer people are around to participate on volunteer rescue squads and fire departments or to volunteer for committees and boards. It is difficult to entice residents to three- or four-hour planning commission meetings after a long day of work and errands involving several different trips.

5.17 Divide and drive: People drive more when land uses are separated.

INTEGRATION

Opportunities for social interaction will be higher in communities where schools, libraries, post offices, convenience stores, services, and homes are located close together. Towns will be more likely to have a rich and diverse population where different types of housing are provided. People will be able to reduce the time spent in their cars when more of their daily stops are in one place. Employers will find employees more productive and business costs lower when they locate near to the residences of a diverse labor force. There are some promising trends that will help to make these opportunities a reality in the future.

CHANGING MARKETS

Residents are indicating that they are looking for neighborhoods with pedestrian orientation and nearby shops and community services. Seventy percent of those polled by the market research firm, American LIVES, in 1996 said that they preferred pedestrian orientation, community gathering places, and nearby shopping. In Chattanooga, Tennessee, a survey showed 30 percent of the respondents would prefer being able to walk to conveniences.[18] Nearly half of the respondents to a Vermont poll said they would like to live in the village or town center "with residences, services, and business in the downtown or village, and working farms or forest land in the rural areas" and where, "going to the post office, shopping, or other errands draws people into the village on a daily basis."[19]

Developers are responding to this market demand. Recently, an 80-unit, six-story residential building was constructed near the waterfront in Burlington, Vermont (**Fig. 5.18**, page 114). Many of the occupants were empty nesters looking for a smaller home with low maintenance close to restaurants, entertainment, shops, and services. An affordable housing project developed in the village of Richmond, Vermont offers units with space for home businesses and a short walk to nearby stores (**Fig. 5.19**, page 114).

The corporate market is changing as well. National retailers and corporate franchises are showing their willingness to fit into mixed-use buildings within town centers (**Fig. 5.20**, page 114). Interviews with industry experts reveal that future opportunities will include "communities that integrate residential, retail and office rather than segregating property uses."[20] Major employers are participating in planning for new mixed use town centers.

5.19 *New affordable housing in Richmond, Vermont, has been built within walking distance of the library, post office, and stores.*

5.18 *New market rate housing in downtown Burlington is located close to restaurants, shops, and services.*

5.20 *A Rite Aid store in downtown Montpelier.*

The Sierra Business Council, whose members include businesses from throughout California's scenic Sierra Nevada region, established planning principles for future growth that include support for mixed use development in compact centers. Adidas America is moving its corporate headquarters from a suburban office park to a central location in an area near downtown Portland, Oregon. The layout of the property will follow a village pattern with three story buildings, a central plaza, pathways that link into the surrounding neighborhood, and sports facilities open to the public.[21] The *New Urban News* in 1999 identified 24 projects involving compact workplace centers with interconnected street networks linked to nearby housing and retail stores.[22] Other corporations and business groups are initiating regional planning projects, affordable housing coalitions, and nonprofit organizations that support sensible growth, including mixed use development.

COMMUNITIES SEEK DIVERSITY

Changing market forces need to be met by changes in community regulations and incentives. The answer to separation is integration, but integration needs to occur in a thoughtful, carefully planned way. Some communities are taking this need very seriously and are creating regulatory provisions that require mixed uses and housing for diverse incomes. Residents of the Town of Essex, Vermont, wanted a new town center that had a pedestrian environment, town offices, a post office, a town square, shops, services, and housing. They developed a plan that laid out future streets and developed design guidelines. When it came time to develop zoning regulations to carry out the plan, they decided to require mixed uses within buildings (**Fig. 5.21**, page 116). The first building constructed has ground floor businesses and low- and moderate-income rental housing upstairs. Two contiguous buildings have also been completed. One has offices downstairs and apartments upstairs, the other is all offices. After a lot of forethought, this town is on its way to creating its dream for a town center.

The Town of Waitsfield, the commercial center for two major ski areas in the scenic Mad River Valley of Vermont, decided to create a plan for its growing commercial center that would encourage mixed uses and a lively, walkable environment. (These efforts were described in Chapter 2.) To insure that projects have multiple uses, the town is now planning to require multi-story buildings. In the meantime, one developer who proposed a one-story bank was convinced to put an apartment upstairs that was occupied for a while by the bank manager (**Fig. 5.22**, page 116). The same developer is now proposing a retail and office building with four large apartments upstairs.

5.21 The town of Essex requires mixed-use developments in its new town center.

5.22 For over 20 years, Waitsfield, Vermont, has been trying to develop a mixed-use center. New development includes a building with a bank downstairs and an apartment upstairs, once occupied by the bank branch manager.

Other communities are examining how they can introduce mixed uses into single-use areas, such as commercial strips, office parks, and residential neighborhoods. In the Town of Stowe, a long commercial strip winds from the village up to the Mt. Mansfield ski resort. Planners in the town grew concerned that the highway tourist zoning district, designated in 1975, was not developing in the pattern they wanted. Large parking lots lined the highway in front of single-use structures, motels, and strip malls. The lovely open spaces along this once scenic corridor that had attracted tourists for many decades were becoming lost to scattered development. To address this problem, the town decided to change its zoning to focus development along the corridor into several mixed use nodes and to protect the remaining open meadows. Within the nodes retail stores, offices, restaurants, and housing will be laid out along a street network lined with sidewalks and street trees. This plan will help reinforce the town's historic settlement pattern of compact, mixed use centers separated by rural countryside (**Fig 5.23**).

In an effort to move away from the exclusivity and isolation of the single-family detached home on two acres in the countryside and provide for the housing needs of a broad section of residents, communities are encouraging mixed housing types and prices in residential neighborhoods and town centers. This involves fixing up deteriorated neighborhoods to attract new households, encouraging affordable housing in new construction projects, and expanding middle- and upper income housing in urban and village centers.

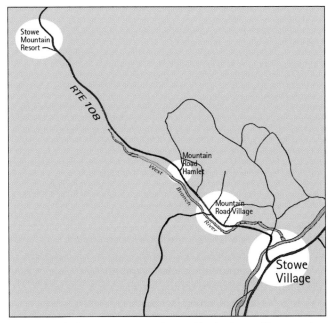

5.23 *Growth along a major tourist corridor in Stowe, Vermont, is directed to a few compact centers.*

5.24 Three historic buildings have been converted to perpetually affordable housing by the Brattleboro Area Community Land Trust. Source: Brattleboro Area Community Land Trust.

With the help of community land trusts, many rural towns and small cities have been able to stabilize and improve the quality of low- and moderate-income areas. These efforts often spur additional investments in the neighborhoods by other property owners, businesses, and employers. The Canal Street neighborhood one block from downtown Brattleboro, Vermont, had a number of historic, but dilapidated buildings that town officials and property owners viewed as suitable for demolition (**Fig. 5.24**). The Brattleboro Community Land Trust spearheaded an effort to rehabilitate many of the buildings into decent, safe, affordable housing for lower income families. When the face lift was under way, one business owner in the neighborhood said the trust had "created a strong sense of place and brought stability back to this residential-business district. It's like night and day!" Also encouraged by the efforts to clean up the neighborhood, the Holstein-Friesian Association, a major local employer, made a commitment to stay, and the refurbishing continued. Other local employers, frustrated by the lack of housing choices for their lower income employees, welcomed the land trust's efforts to develop more units in the town.

Another approach to bringing different types of housing units together in one place is to require that a certain percentage of all units in new residential projects be affordable to low- and moderate-income families through inclusionary zoning. For 10 years the City of Burlington has had an inclusionary zoning provision that requires developers of projects over five units[23] to make 15 to 25 percent of their units available for affordable housing.[24] A density bonus is offered to help developers finance the afford-

5.25 *These affordable housing units in Burlington, Vermont, were required under inclusionary zoning.*

able units.[25] A total of 100, mostly owner-occupied, low- and moderate-income units have been provided through this mechanism. (**Fig. 5.25**)

In smaller communities, which typically lack large housing projects suitable for inclusionary zoning, smaller steps can be taken to diversify housing. Vermont planning law requires towns to allow accessory housing units with single-family homes for relatives, people over 55 years of age, and the disabled.[26] Some communities have taken this law further and permitted accessory apartments for any household. Other communities allow accessory buildings, such as garages or carriage houses, to be converted to housing provided parking and sanitary facilities can be accommodated.

PUBLIC POLICY SUPPORTS INTEGRATION

Local, state, and federal officials around the country are reexamining their public investment practices and making changes in order to improve the quality of community life and prevent sprawl. These steps will greatly assist the diversification of uses and activities in communities. For example, communities are looking at abandoned school sites for elderly housing, libraries, and other civic needs. Small towns that have outgrown town offices and library space are locating the new buildings on vacant land in or next to villages where they would like to develop a town center. State school construction standards are being examined to see if their require-ments for recreational space, building layout, and the number of acres per student hinder rehabilitation. Bills have been introduced in Congress to require the U.S. Postal Service adhere to community plans in its locational decisions. Public investment decision makers are now beginning to focus on bringing uses back together, not separating them as they did in the past.

Steps by communities and state and federal governments are needed if the barriers to community life posed by separation of uses are to be over-come. There are signs that these steps are being taken. Private forces, too, are being redirected toward this purpose. Market studies show that people want a wide range of choices in housing types and locations. Businesses have demonstrated renewed interest in locating in downtowns. Major employers are participating in mixed-use development projects. All of these steps will help reduce time spent driving, promote communities that offer a wide range of housing types, goods, and services for their residents and work forces, and overcome the isolation of people from each other and their communities.

NOTES

1. Federal Housing Administration. "Successful Subdivisions," *Land Planning Bulletin No. 1*, U.S. Government Printing Office, Washington, D.C., 1940, p. 10.

2. Patricia S. Hu and Jennifer R. Young. *Summary of Travel Trends, 1995 Nationwide Personal Transportation Survey*, U.S. Department of Transportation, December 1999.

3. U.S. Bureau of Transportation Statistics, U.S. Department of Transportation. *National Transportation Statistics, 1999*, p. 43. Also: U.S. Bureau of the Census, *U.S. Census of Population*, 1980 and 1995. A 1992 study, *Travel Behavior Issues in the 90's*, by the U.S. Department of Transportation, found that the increase in trip lengths explained 35 percent of the growth in driving.

4. In larger metropolitan areas, dispersal into the suburbs began with street cars and rail service, well before the advent of the automobile.

5. St. Albans Group and Wal-Mart Stores, Inc. No 6F0471-EB, 1995 WL 404828, at 1 (Vermont Environmental Board, June 27, 1995).

6. *In re* Wal-Mart Stores, 9 Vt.L.Wk.233, 702 A.2nd 397 (1997).

7. Federal Housing Administration. "Successful Subdivisions," *Land Planning Bulletin No. 1*, U.S. Government Printing Office, Washington, D.C., 1940, p. 14.

8. In 2001, a new downtown grocery store was under construction with financial support from the city and its residents.

9. According to the American Travel Survey, lower income people are less likely to use personal automobiles for their travel needs and are more likely to use intercity bus service than people of higher incomes.

10. National Association of Local Government Environmental Professionals. *Profiles of Business Leadership on Smart Growth*, Washington, D.C. 1999, p. 27.

11. Ibid., p. 78.

12. According to data from the U.S. Census Bureau, new homes are less likely to be located near multiunit housing, businesses, and institutions than older homes are. The bureau's 1997 American Housing Survey provided data on the percentage of all single-family detached housing that was located within 300 feet of other single-family housing, apartments, commerce and institutions, and open space. Similar data were provided for new single-family detached housing. The data show that outside metropolitan statistical areas, the percentage of new housing next to apartments is 32.5 percent lower than that for all units, and the percentage next to commerce and institutions is 39.9 percent lower than that for all housing. In these same areas, the percentage of new single-family housing that is near open space is 31.1 percent higher than the percentage for all homes. Source: U.S. Census Bureau, *Current Housing Reports*, Series H150/97, *American Housing Survey of the United States*.

13. National Association of Home Builders. *Smart Growth, Building Better Places to Live, Work and Play,* Washington, D.C., 1999, p. 16.

14. Vermont Forum on Sprawl. *Exploring Sprawl #6: Economic, Social, and Land Use Trends Related to Sprawl,* Burlington, Vermont, August 1999.

15. Surface Transportation Policy Project. *High Mileage Moms,* January 13, 2000.

16. Hu and Young, p. 13.

17. Ibid., p. 214.

18. Melissa Heron. "Brave New World," *Builder,* July 1998, p. 110.

19. Vermont Forum on Sprawl. *Exploring Sprawl #1: Vermonters' Attitudes on Sprawl,* Burlington, Vermont, February 1999.

20. PricewaterhouseCoopers LLP and Lend Lease Real Estate Investments, Inc. *Emerging Trends in Real Estate,* New York, October 1999, p. 7.

21. Diane Dulken, "Foot Traffic," *Planning,* June 1999, pp. 16-17.

22. "Employment Centers That Function Like Neighborhoods," *New Urban News,* May-June 1999, pp. 1 and 3.

23. Reuse or conversion of nonresidential properties for 10 or more residential units must comply with the inclusionary zoning provisions of the city of Burlington.

24. The percentage of all units that must be inclusionary varies between rental and owner occupied units, the location of the units in the city, and sales prices of the units developed.

25. The size of the density bonus varies by zoning district.

26. Title 24, Vermont Statutes Annotated §4406 (4)(D).

Perched up on a hilltop above Montpelier, Vermont, surrounded by trees, and reached by a winding access road, is a large office building (**Fig. 6.2**). This is the headquarters of an insurance company, National Life of Vermont. Although it lies within the city of Montpelier, everything about the complex—the design of the building, the setting, and the approach to it—sets it apart from what goes on further down the hill. The downtown buildings share space along a network of public streets. National Life exists outside that network, in a world unto itself. Unlike the shops, offices, and other businesses downtown, which hug the main thoroughfares, this building is isolated. No one passes by the front door on his daily rounds. It occupies the private domain, not the public realm.

The architect Peter Calthorpe describe conflicting impulses in all of us when he wrote of "a defensive exclusionary desire for retreat and an optimistic desire to create community." In the past, the built environment reflected a balance of these two conflicting impulses. This balance is reflected in towns laid out in the 19th and the early part of the 20th centuries. The public realm—represented by schools, parks, streets, libraries, town halls, and other places that "determine the quality of our shared world and express the value we assign to community"—was nurtured and maintained. But lately, in contemporary design, our private wishes have dominated. We lavish more care and attention on our private spaces than on our public ones. The urge for retreat and control, not the urge for community, sets the tone of the modern suburb.[1] And as the public realm grows more impoverished, the need to escape to the private domain increases.

This emphasis on privacy is becoming more evident as the contemporary land settlement pattern reaches into rural America. The layout of streets and the siting of buildings in recent growth areas often reveal an obsession with privacy and controlled access. Office parks such as National Life, shopping malls, gated communities and other planned residential developments built outside the public street network, even rural homes on 10-acre lots, provide varying measures of insulation from the community at large.

As a nation, we used to be good at nurturing public life. We built our towns in a pattern that helped community to thrive. This chapter will explore how we have shifted away from that tradition, how our obsession with privacy and neglect of public space are reflected in recent development. It will show how the location and design of our businesses and homes increases our isolation and hurts our community life, and how the public realm of small towns is increasingly shaped by private interests. Our earlier tradition of public space-making is discussed in the second half of the chapter, which describes how physical form can convey a sense of identity and belonging and how altering the pattern of new development can restore balance between our public and private realms.

6.2 *Although it is within the boundaries of Montpelier, everything about the National Life office complex (its design, setting, and approach) sets it apart from what goes on farther down the hill.*

ENCLAVES

Like many successful large companies, National Life has a long history of growth and expansion. Between 1858 and 1921 it moved five times, from a former residence to a rented second floor, to a three-story building, then to an even larger, six-story building occupying a whole block. Each move accommodated the company's expanding workforce and symbolized its increasing prominence in the community of Montpelier. **Figures 6.3 to 6.7** show this series of buildings. Each structure reflects the architectural style of the age. This is a company that prided itself on moving with the times. So it's not surprising that when National Life had outgrown its 1921 quarters, it followed the latest trend in architectural design. In 1957, that meant not only a radically different building style but also a very different context. It moved out of downtown to the nearby hilltop.

Note in the historic photos how the first five National Life buildings were set on city streets. Their front doors were not more than 20 steps off the sidewalk. They were part of the fabric of downtown, visible and accessible to the whole community. But the company's most recent building reflects a different approach. It is removed from the city and sits alone on a large lawn in the middle of some woods (**Fig. 6.8**). The entrance is not a few steps from the main streets of Montpelier but a mile up a long road with no sidewalks. Unlike its predecessors, this building is not on the way to anywhere else. Its location filters out those who belong from those who do not. National Life may or may not have wanted to convey exclusivity with this building, but the fact that it was harder to reach made it so. By

physically removing its workforce from downtown, it pulled away from the community of Montpelier. The new National Life is visible not from the downtown but from the interstate highway. It traded a presence on the street for a more distant visibility.

National Life's move wasn't unusual. The steady progression of businesses and homes from city center to suburb, from suburb to exurb, is illustrated in Chapter Three. The image of a modern corporate headquarters set apart from a 19th century downtown symbolizes the shift from the center to the edge, but it also conveys something more: a retreat away from the community into an enclave. Moving up the hill provided National Life with more than space and scenery. It gave the company more privacy and control over its immediate environment. Unlike the buildings downtown, which front public streets controlled by the city of Montpelier, National Life sits on a large parcel of private land. It has control over the road that leads to it and the parking lots that surround it. The space between the building and its neighbors provides the company with a cushion of privacy and a measure of control that it didn't have with its earlier buildings.

Businesses and home buyers move out to the edge for many reasons. In the 1950s, privacy and control may have been an attractive side benefit of leaving downtown. But since that time, as we have moved farther and farther out, we have grown accustomed to it. We expect a certain level of privacy and want to control our contact with others, shaping our communities to achieve these ends.

6.3-6.9 *National Life Insurance Company headquarters. The company's first five offices were located on the main streets of downtown Montpelier. Source: Courtesy Vermont Historical Society.*

6.6 *1891-1921*

6.5 *1873-1891*

6.3-6.4 *The company occupied these two buildings between 1858 and 1873.*

6.8 *In 1960 the firm removed itself from the bustle of downtown and set its new building on a grassy expanse about a mile away.*

6.7 *1921-1960*

To see how form and layout can control access and reinforce privacy, take a look at a typical contemporary subdivision built at the edge of town. Like many new developments, the one shown in **Fig. 6.9** stands off on its own, surrounded by fields, and is arranged around a self-contained street network. This is not a gated community. There are no guards or "keep out" signs. But the design of this place produces the same effect. As with the National Life complex, there are only a few entrances and no through streets, which means that no one will be "just passing through." Apart from occasional service people, only a resident or a resident's guest would have a reason to enter.

There is much in this neighborhood to appeal to our urge for privacy and control. Each house is an enclave within an enclave. The large front and side yards provide a cushion against unwanted social contact with neighbors. And the location of the garages adds to the isolation. In a more compact neighborhood, the simple act of parking the car and walking to the front door is often an opportunity to greet or acknowledge other people on the street. Distances are short and face-to-face contact and conversations are possible. But in this neighborhood, with its attached garages and remote controlled doors, even the short walk from car to house is made in completely private space. Driving directly into the house eliminates the possibility of that driveway conversation. In this contemporary development pattern, residents have more control over their territory; they encounter fewer outsiders and have fewer unanticipated social interactions than residents of urban neighborhoods. This is the appeal of an

enclave. It frees us from day-to-day social conflict.[2]

But the drawback of this type of neighborhood layout is that it doesn't help to nurture relationships between people. By nature, an enclave establishes an "us" versus "them" attitude, making fellow citizens into outsiders or intruders rather than neighbors. Enclaves can breed intolerance by limiting the insiders' ability to establish bonds with a larger community. The social contract that holds our society together depends on social contact. Privatized neighborhoods limit social contact and narrow the bonds of mutual responsibility between citizens.[3]

An obsession with privacy also prevents people from enjoying their neighbors and feeling a sense of belonging. If most of the land and buildings are private, as they are in this subdivision, there's no neutral ground for informal conversations and chance meetings. There is no park, no corner store, not even a sidewalk where two neighbors might run into each other. Because the environment is meant for driving, not walking, people tend to stick to their cars (**Fig. 6.10**). It's hard to connect with someone who is encased in a vehicle and moving 30 miles an hour. When all of the resources available to build a neighborhood are put into private amenities such as large lots, big climate-controlled houses, garages, and wide roads, there is little left for sidewalks, street trees, greens, or open fields. This is typical of a trend that has occurred for the good part of a century. As a nation we've become skilled at creating private space, but we've fallen short on creating places to gather. Our dwellings have grown and become more luxurious while our community spaces have shrunk. Gone are the

6.9 The layout and design of many modern subdivisions reinforce their isolation. Their cul-de-sacs, front yards, and attached garages provide a buffer against unwanted social contact. New neighborhoods are well endowed with private space, but they lack sidewalks, street trees, greens, and the other shared amenities.

6.10 Another subdivision offers a different design, but a similar choice. Here, the houses are close together but oriented to the back yard. The only entrance to the front of these houses is through the automatic garage door, which opens only to the driver of the car. The street becomes a lonely and boring place with few windows facing it and no people about.

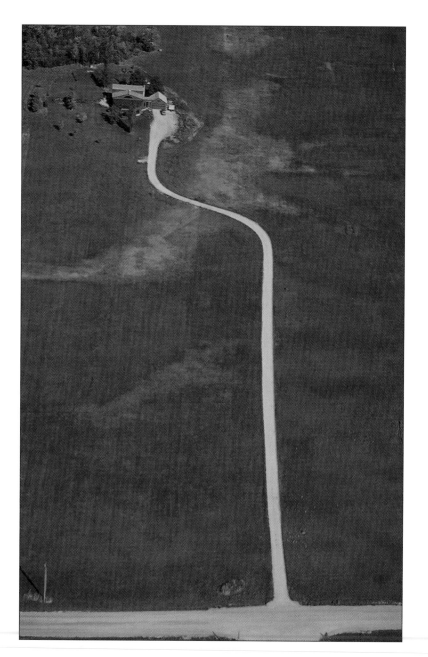

6.11 The ultimate enclave: a 10-acre plot.

6.12 Houses plopped down in a rural setting don't necessarily belong to a rural culture. As rural towns grow into suburbs and their economy shifts away from local resources, that culture fades, along with the connections that sustain communities.

informal gathering places of the past—the store, the green, the soda foun-
tain, and the barbershop—places to drop by and hang out in. Now, houses
are large and well appointed, but they exist in areas with few or no public
facilities.[4] In contemporary subdivision design, private space rules. It is
allocated more space and receives more investment than the public areas
shared by the community as a whole.

Except, of course, for the roadway, which is usually quite ample. In a
typical subdivision, streets are at least 30 feet wide (**Fig. 6.10**). Although
the disconnected street network ensures that these streets will receive very
limited traffic, they are scaled to handle the speed and volume of a highway. In this case space and money are devoted to a public facility, but it is
one that serves a single function: the smooth and easy movement of cars.
The travel lanes are wide, curves are gentle, on-street parking is restricted,
and sidewalks are limited to one side of the street. The design reveals a
bias toward a private, insulated form of travel and against more public
ones such as walking and biking. And when a street is treated as a single-
purpose utility, it fails to provide the high-quality public space that
encourages neighborly interaction.[5]

In cities and villages, where people live close together, walk, and take
public transportation, they can't avoid each other easily. To handle potential conflict they must know rules for social behavior such as greeting people, waiting in lines, sharing public space. They grow accustomed to
accommodation, to negotiation. For the exurban dweller, the rules of social
interaction need to be much fewer in number.[6]

Perhaps this is why the 10-acre-plus lot is the ultimate enclave, the
defensive, exclusionary desire for retreat at its most pronounced. The
owner of the home in **Fig. 6.11** need not be concerned about unwanted
social contact. The chance encounter with a neighbor, the casual conversation with a passerby is not going to happen here. This house is surrounded by an envelope of private property that keeps outsiders out.[7]

But isn't living out in the country on a big spread what rural life is all
about? Isn't *not* having neighbors the whole idea? Isolation holds a certain
appeal for contemporary home buyers fleeing suburbia. To them, neighbors often represent the sprawl they left behind. But what suburban
refugees often overlook, as they light on 10-acre lots, is an equally strong
need for community—a connection with other people. This connection is
difficult to sustain while living a modern suburban lifestyle in the middle
of a field. Although houses such as those in **Fig. 6.12** may exist in a rural
setting they haven't grown out of a rural culture.

In traditional rural culture people live far apart, but neighbors have all
kinds of bonds that strengthen community. The act of working the land
ties individuals to the place in a profound way and gives a sense of
belonging. Cooperation and negotiation is essential to resolve disputes
over common boundaries or other issues that cross property lines. Rural
residents often have local roots and a connection to the community. And
the shared enterprise of running the town requires interaction and common purpose. In rural towns volunteers shoulder much of the responsibility of government, from managing the school to staffing the rescue squad.

This brings people of different opinions and backgrounds together.

As rural towns grow into suburbs, and the economy shifts away from locally based agriculture and resources, this culture fades, and with it, many of the connections between people that sustain community. Newcomers usually don't work the land and often make their living in another town. They don't have a history in town that helps them understand their neighbors. As the population increases, the sense of community that comes from being in a small group, of "knowing everybody," is lost. Town government becomes less personal and participatory. Without these ties that bind, it's more difficult to feel a sense of belonging and a connection to a group larger than the family unit. The public realm of traditional rural culture exists in social relationships more often than in physical space. Because contemporary life is undermining the structure of those relationships, it is vital to create a physical pattern that can reinforce them. And the lone house in the center of a large lot at the end of a long driveway isn't a pattern that helps build relationships.

DE FACTO TOWN MAKERS

Enclaves often appear when communities have handed the role of town making over to private interests. When communities fail to plan for growth in a comprehensive, far-sighted way, they abdicate their responsibility to shape the public realm. An example is the responsibility to plan street networks. Streets are the single most important component of public space. A comprehensive street network, like those found in traditional cities, forms channels that connect people and provides acres of linear common space. Yet rarely these days does a town take on the responsibility of planning an interconnected and pedestrian-friendly street network. Instead, it leaves the task of locating roads to fate and the cost of building them to developers.

Figure 6.13 shows what Jericho, Vermont, looked like in the 1930s, when it was a farming town. As it grew into a suburb, Jericho allowed land to be subdivided incrementally. The large farm parcels were broken into smaller building lots, and streets were built to provide access. Over the years, as each developer focused on his individual subdivision, he created a street or two within the boundaries of the parcel. By 1988, a disconnected street pattern had emerged (**Fig. 6.14**). The black lines outline the house lots and the yellow lines show the new streets. Most are dead ends. Some are loop roads. None of them connects with other subdivisions. If the town had taken it upon itself to draw out a connected street system *before* the land was developed, each parcel could have been laid out to reinforce that system. Instead, it got 10 separate auto-dependent enclaves. With no official plan to determine inter-neighborhood connections, private

6.13 Jericho, Vermont, in 1937.

6.14 Over the years, as each builder focused on a single subdivision, streets were built to serve individual developments but not neighboring ones. By 1988, most of the streets were dead ends or loop roads. None connected with other subdivisions. The black lines outline house lots; yellow lines show new streets.

developers became de facto transportation planners for the community.

Roads play an important role in connecting people and strengthening community. They're also a prime spur for development. So the placement of new roads is crucial in determining where growth will and will not go. As noted in earlier chapters, other types of infrastructure are instrumental as well. This is why decisions about where infrastructure goes are a matter of public policy. Yet towns often relinquish their authority to whoever is willing to pay for it. For example, when a developer offers to extend a sewer or water line to serve his proposed shopping center along the highway outside town, a cash-strapped community may be tempted by the "free" infrastructure. Once in place, the sewer and water lines attract more businesses. If the town didn't want strip development in the first place, the new pipes were no bargain. As in Jericho, private developers were playing the role that should have been embraced by local government: setting policy on how and where the town grows.

PLACELESSNESS

No two towns are exactly alike. Each has a particular street layout and arrangement of buildings, shaped over a particular period of time in a particular geography by a particular population. The dynamic forces of place, time, and culture work to create endless variations on the theme of city, town, or village.

At least they used to. In another era—when buildings were constructed of local materials, regional architectural styles dominated, businesses were locally owned, and engineering technology was limited—local culture and geography played a larger role in the shaping of towns. Roads snaked and dipped, buildings were added onto, and added onto again, signs were designed one at a time. Barre, Vermont, looked somewhat similar to nearby Montpelier, but not quite like Hudson, New York, and a whole lot different from Flagstaff, Arizona. Regional style prevailed, but local variations provided uniqueness. With a similar physical geography and building stock, Barre and Montpelier seem like twins. But a closer look reveals that they are by no means identical. Different industries and populations in each community created two different variations on the theme of 19th century central Vermont town.

At the beginning of the 21st century, however, the subtle differences between places are fading and the bigger regional distinctions hardly exist. The lament that "everywhere looks like somewhere else" is increasingly true. The newer parts of Barre, Vermont, *are* beginning to look like sections of Flagstaff, Arizona. The constraints that produced a quirky variety of places in the past are long gone. Building materials can be imported from anywhere. Hills can be flattened and streams relocated. We can transform the landscape with greater ease and place there whatever meets our budget or strikes our fancy, whether it's Georgia pine or Italian marble. Technical innovations, greater mechanization, and the global economy all make it easy for a building plan drawn up at a corporate headquarters in Illinois to be applied over and over again, in Kentucky, or Oregon, or any other site across the country.

In a civic sense, community springs from identification with a place. The stronger the sense of place, the more likely residents will identify with it. And that sense of place comes from the feeling that their town is somehow distinct from other places. A century ago, the intersection in **Fig. 6.15** contained a church and two buildings designed by local architects. One of these is seen in a previous chapter (**Fig. 3.22**, see page 53). This was an entirely unique intersection at the heart of Morrisville, Vermont. Now only the church remains. The two missing buildings were replaced with structures that, while evocative of their time—late 20th century gas station design—don't convey any sense of the place that is Morrisville. The same rectangular boxes that float above these gas pumps also float above pumps in thousands of Citgo and Gulf stations across the nation. This is an example of corporate franchise design that homogenizes the visual character of place by imposing uniform design. The horizontal nature of the canopies, the scale of the signs, the bold colors, the large setback, and the overblown lighting are completely unrelated to the context of this village.

The essence of franchise design is sameness. It offers customers famil-

6.15 *Corporate designs can homogenize the visual character of a place by imposing a uniform look.*

iarity, wherever in the world they may be. Logos, color schemes, building shape, and even site layouts must be identical to reassure consumers of the corporate presence. In the process of conveying this message, corporate design often overwhelms the public spaces of small towns and villages, appropriating the public realm for private purposes. Citgo and Gulf achieved their goals on the main intersection of Morrisville, but at a cost to the community's sense of place and aesthetic character.

Anonymous franchise design that dominates public space. Remote and insulated houses. Inwardly focused corporate campuses. Disconnected streets: These are the signs, visible in contemporary development patterns, that the balance between our private and public selves has tilted sharply. In the built environment, privatism, or the attitude of being uncommitted to anything beyond one's immediate interests, has won out over a more optimistic desire to create community.

However, just because we've neglected community recently doesn't mean that we can discard it. Despite our obsession with privacy, we are social beings who need contact and support from others. What Jane Jacobs called "a web of public respect and trust, and a resource in a time of personal or neighborhood need"[8] is just as important to the good life as a cozy retreat. A healthy community depends on social relationships and requires settings in which to nurture those relationships. Communal space, where people can gather, is needed to form community. "Just as it is difficult to imagine the concept of *family* independent of the home, it is near-impossible to imagine *community* independent of the town square or the local pub."[9]

COMMON GROUND

Streets and public spaces are the building blocks of the public realm, but how do they contribute to community life? In addition to their functional role of providing a gathering place, they play a symbolic role in defining a community's identity. An understandable street network provides residents and visitors alike with a strong sense of orientation. It's easy to find your way around. And when you know the territory, you feel more at home. Well-defined public spaces such as greens, squares, or Main Streets provide not only a place to gather but also a community identity and a sense of place.

One such traditional pattern is found in the village of Enosburg, Vermont (**Fig. 6.16**). In **Fig. 6.17**, the streets and greens of Enosburg have been masked to reveal how these corridors and squares organize the buildings around them and provide connections. They create a coherent and memorable pattern that is easy to navigate within but is unique to Enosburg. The spaces are ordered in a way typical of New England villages. A main shopping street forms a spine along which the central green sits. On a quieter back street, a second green centers a neighborhood. A mid-block sidewalk connects this residential green to Main Street, increasing its accessibility to the whole community and reinforcing its public aspect.

On a hill above downtown Barre, Vermont, is a settlement that stands in stark contrast with the National Life building and the subdivision shown earlier. Unlike those developments, this neighborhood (**Fig. 6.18**, page 138) is not an enclave. It was designed to invite entry, to encourage

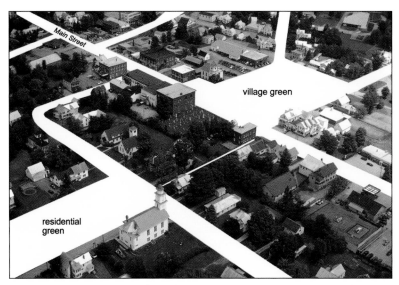

6.16 Street networks that are clear and understandable give residents and visitors alike a sense of orientation.

6.17 The streets and greens of Enosburg, Vermont, have been masked to show how its corridors and squares organize the buildings around them.

social interaction, and to connect its inhabitants with the larger community. Because it was built in a different time, it is well endowed with the diversity and physical infrastructure that encourages community.

This hillside neighborhood is close to the city center. It has the usual supply of single-family homes found in any residential district plus a less-than-usual collection of apartment buildings, offices, and neighborhood businesses. Its location and diversity are two reasons this area is not an enclave. A third is its form. One can enter this neighborhood at any one of seven intersections and once in, can make direct connections to every street. The green at the center of the neighborhood and the regular gridded layout of streets make it easy to get oriented and remember what's where. Closely spaced houses, narrow front lawns, porches, and sidewalks create a setting for informal conversations on the streets (**Fig. 6.20**). The green serves as the neighborhood's communal front yard. It is intricately joined to the center of town through a series of public spaces, which include streets, sidewalks, and greens. **Figure 6.19** highlights these public spaces, showing how they provide connections between the downtown on the right and the neighborhood on the left.

There are several public buildings along the streets between the hill and downtown. A resident walking from any house to Main Street strolls past his neighbors' front doors, through a green, past offices, social clubs, and churches, and into the heart of the city. And because the neighborhood has a diverse array of housing types, chances are good that the people he meets along the way aren't just like him. This is the physical infrastructure

that creates a comfortable environment for pedestrians and brings people face to face. It allows for the social contact that helps a community sustain its social contract.[10]

6.18 A mix of single-family houses, apartment buildings, and scattered businesses provide diversity in this neighborhood in Barre, Vermont. The whole neighborhood is located within walking distance of downtown, noted at the right of the photo.

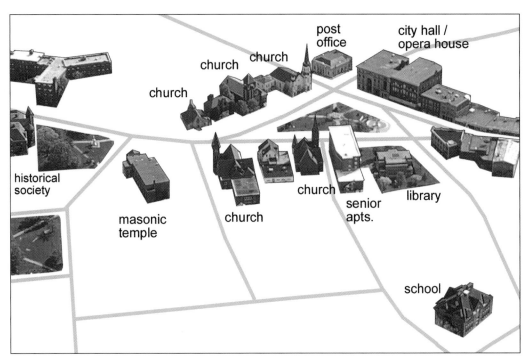

6.19 This diagram replicates the area outlined in white in Fig. 6.18. Note the public buildings and spaces (streets, sidewalks, and greens) that connect the neighborhood with the city center.

6.20 Neighborhood features include short front yards, sidewalks, and tall trees.

139

RESTORING BALANCE

Americans clearly value privacy and control. Businesses need to control their workspace and express themselves in the marketplace. The challenge is to satisfy those needs while strengthening the public realm and increasing the opportunities for community life. Part of the solution lies in design: creating private space that fulfills all the requirements of modern life while contributing to an overall pattern of high-quality public space.

An example of this is to redesign and develop alternatives to the ubiquitous cul-de-sac. Cul-de-sac streets are an emblem of sprawl. With their auto-dependent and isolated form, they represent the essence of suburbia. A subdivision made up of long dead-end streets has no describable pattern or identity. It makes outsiders feel at a loss. And it's no fun to walk around in because there's nowhere to go. But cul-de-sacs are extremely popular because they contain little traffic, offering safe and quiet street space to residents. On a cul-de-sac, people tend to take over the street, using it for play and other social needs. It's possible to distill its better qualities into a form that supports rather than discourages community interaction. A more compact, urban form of the cul-de-sac—a "court"—can offer residents a quiet street that encourages contact between neighbors and is integrated into a larger community.[11]

An example is shown in **Fig. 6.21**. This short street is located in a city neighborhood close to schools, stores, parks, and other services. Because it was recently built in the middle of an already developed block, there was no chance of making this a through street. Like the cul-de-sacs of suburbia, it doesn't lead anywhere, but it does adhere to and extend the existing

street network. It fits the pattern already established in the neighborhood. Houses are aligned in the same grid, they are close together, and they sit up on the street. After entering this little street, it's clear that the houses are modern but the pattern is familiar. It seems a part of the existing neighborhood and not a separate enclave. Unlike a typical cul-de-sac, the houses here are close together and face each other across a short distance. As a result, the street is an enclosed outdoor living room rather than a no man's land. If dead end streets are short, if they fit within the context of a traditional urban pattern and are within easy reach of downtown, they can add to the public life of a community.

Another urban alternative to the cul-de-sac is the quiet back street. This type of street, often found in small villages, runs parallel to a busier road, connecting with it at two or more points. Through traffic stays off, giving the street a more peaceful atmosphere for residents and offering a pleasant alternative route for pedestrians and bicyclists (**Fig. 6.22**). New back streets can be grafted onto existing networks, as was done in a small-lot subdivision in Stowe, Vermont (**Fig. 6.23**).

Other design approaches can strengthen the public realm of towns and cities as well. One is traffic calming, a technique of physically modifying streets to slow traffic. The hallmark of an inclusive, open neighborhood is an interconnected street network. But often it's not all that appealing to residents wary of through traffic. Traffic calming is being used successfully throughout the country to restore the safety and quiet of neighborhood streets. By narrowing the street at intersections, installing speed humps,

NOTES

1. Peter Calthorpe. *The Next American Metropolis*, New York, Princeton Architectural Press, 1993, pp. 23-38.

2. Constance Perin. *Everything in its Place: Social Order and Land Use in America*, Princeton, New Jersey, Princeton University Press, 1977, pp. 86-89.

3. Edward J. Blakely and Mary G. Snyder. *Fortress America: Gated Communities in the United States*, Washington, D.C., Brookings Institution and Cambridge, Massachusetts, Lincoln Institute of Land Policy, 1997, pp. 138-139.

4. Ray Oldenburg. *The Great Good Place*, New York, Marlowe and Company, 1989, p. 18 and p. 214.

5. Calthorpe, p. 37.

6. Perin, p. 89.

7. Perin, p. 86.

8. Jane Jacobs. *The Death and Life of Great American Cities*, New York, Random House, 1961, p. 56.

9. Andres Duany, Elizabeth Plater-Zyberk, and Jeff Speck. *Suburban Nation: The Rise of Sprawl and the Decline of the American Dream*, New York, North Point Press, 2000, p. 60.

10. Blakely and Snyder, p. 3.

11. Michael Southworth and Eran Ben-Joseph. *Streets and the Shaping of Towns and Cities*, New York, McGraw Hill, 1997, pp. 120-125.

12. Oldenburg, p. ix and p. 14.

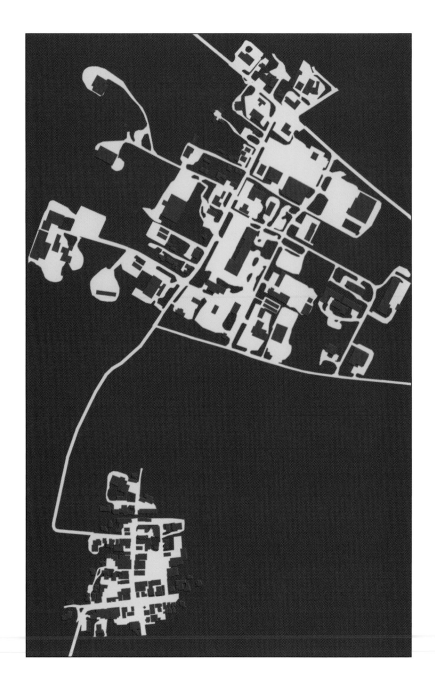

7.2 Morristown is bigger than
Morrisville, and so are its buildings,
lots, and streets. Buildings are shown
in red, paved areas in yellow.

NEEDING AND WANTING MORE

Figure 7.2 tells the story of two places that look very different even though they are only a short distance apart. The contrast between the two areas epitomizes the changing scale of settlement in many rural communities. Historic Morrisville, at the bottom of the image, contains small buildings lined up along the street. Paved lots behind the buildings enable business-es to share parking. Many different uses exist within a short walking dis-tance. In the more recently developed commercial and industrial hub of Morristown, at the top of the image, we see large footprints of buildings, each surrounded by asphalt, accommodating driveways, parked cars, and space for trucks. Each building is isolated from the others—separated by vast, inhospitable paved areas.

These two places reflect the different scales of development at the turn of the last century and today. In Morrisville, as more retail space was needed to accommodate a larger range of goods or as population growth required a bigger meeting hall or a larger school, buildings were expanded upstairs or out the back. Taller buildings replaced short buildings. New buildings filled gaps along the street. Most needs for expansion were met within or adjacent to the village until the automobile made other locations more feasible.

In the 1960s, commercial building trends called for one-story layouts, large aisles, high ceilings, and on-site parking. Long, flat buildings and lots of asphalt were required—both of which were hard to provide in the compact village. A large expanse of farmland was set aside to meet the demand for space. With so much commercial property available at an inexpensive price, there was little incentive to use the land efficiently. Therefore, large buildings surrounded by parking were spread out on the landscape—a sharp contrast to compact Morrisville.

The scale of homes has also grown dramatically. Once a one- or two-bedroom home would suffice for an entire family. Now homeowners often require one bedroom and one bathroom for each person plus additional rooms for other specialized needs: cooking, eating, playing, working, laun-dry, reading. A 5,000-square-foot lot (a little more than an eighth of an acre) was once a typical single-family lot size. Today's rural families look for two-acre, five-acre, and 10-acre lots.

As our homes and businesses and the lots that accommodate them have grown, so has the scale of our settlements. Needs that once were met within the small center of a community now consume acres and acres of land surrounding the community and beyond. We see this in shopping centers with large parking lots, office parks where each building has its own yard, and homes with massive lawns. For over a century, Morrisville added people and buildings in small incremental steps. In Morristown, on the other hand, large imprints across the landscape signified a dramatic shift in the scale of development.

We can measure the changes in scale from our own experiences. A small store is more intimate, and we can easily feel comfortable there. A big store is more challenging, and we can feel lost at times. The desirabili-ty of walking or driving is often determined by the scale of development. A walk by a small shop is quick; a walk by a big box store seems endless.

To drive between shops in a downtown seems ridiculous; to drive between big box stores is the norm. The downtown has a pedestrian scale; the big box store area has an automobile scale.

As we move away from the pedestrian to the automobile scale of development, we consume land at an ever-growing rate. Nationally, population grew by 16 percent between 1982 and 1997 while developed land grew by 40 percent—about two and one half times the rate of population growth.[1]

People around the country are questioning this consumptive pattern of growth and saying, "Enough!" Individuals, communities, planners, and developers are looking for alternatives that support smaller scale development in town centers and in new growth areas. They are finding ways to build better places in smaller spaces.

COMMERCIAL SPACE

A 53,000-square-foot supermarket in Morristown, Vermont, with its immense, flat building and its huge parking area, renders the nearby downtown obsolete and dooms the deteriorating farm across the street (**Fig. 7.3**). Grocery store, drug store, clothing store, and department store goods, once available on Main Street, now are found under one roof in big boxes out on the highway, often at lower prices, in larger volumes, and with more convenient parking. Unable to compete, smaller stores in nearby downtowns and villages close as stores at the edges grow larger and larger.

Why are new stores so big? By offering "one-stop shopping"—that is, a selection of every item that a consumer might wish to purchase—often at low prices, these businesses are able to draw people from other stores in the surrounding area and expand their market area by many miles. By providing a large selection of goods and selling in big volumes within an efficient store layout that minimizes labor needs, business is conducted at a lower cost. National companies' prescriptions for building layout and design dictate large, flat rectangles. Business economics show that this pattern makes good financial sense: developers have found that the bigger the building, the lower its square foot costs for leasing.[2] The bigger the box, the bigger the parking lot, and the wider the roads that lead to it

Why can't these uses fit into our existing town and village centers? One reason is that the huge buildings could dramatically alter the character of the centers. While the goods and services could be offered on more than one floor and, thus, fit better, most proprietors no longer are interested in this layout. They prefer to have everything on one level. With "just in time

7.3 A 53,000-square-foot grocery store at the edge of Morristown dwarfs a farm across the street.

7.4 *Big industrial buildings on large lots along an interstate highway. The dotted lines show unused land on each parcel.*

7.5 *Big industrial buildings on small lots next to downtown Springfield, Vermont.*

delivery," the parking and truck loading spaces required by these businesses are hard to fit into the small lots available in downtowns. The shopping activity generated by these stores can snarl traffic on narrow village streets. Finally, local permit standards make such accommodations difficult.

It is not just the scale of buildings that has increased dramatically. The size of the lots on which these structures are located also has grown. The buildings actually take up a small percentage of the total lot size. The remainder is used for parking, landscaping and generous setbacks from the road and adjoining structures (**Fig. 7.4**). Zoning regulations encourage these patterns.

In Chittenden County, Vermont, zoning regulations for retail stores, services, and offices actually mandate sprawl development patterns. Commercial buildings in suburban locations use only five to 10 percent of their lots while buildings in nearby downtowns use 80 to 100 percent of theirs.[3]

Growth in the size of lots and of industrial buildings also is encouraged by zoning. In Chittenden County, industrial buildings outside of urban centers often are not permitted to exceed 10 percent to 25 percent of a lot. Required lot sizes for industrial buildings are large—often larger than those for commercial buildings. Communities are literally zoning out traditional patterns of settlement, such as compact industries in urban centers (**Fig. 7.5**).

The combination of large buildings and restrictive zoning standards is adding up to a dramatic increase in the amount of land used for business and industry outside of town centers.

7.6 *A neighborhood of houses on small lots, built close to a tree-lined street in St. Albans City, Vermont.*

7.7 *A newer neighborhood in nearby St. Albans Town, with houses spaced far apart and set well back from the street.*

7.8 *More houses can fit on the interconnected streets in an older neighborhood.*

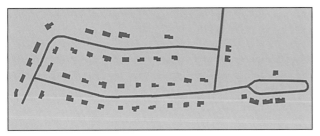

7.9 *Zoning that requires large lot sizes produce fewer houses in the newer neighborhood.*

DOMESTIC SPACE

Our appetite has grown not only for commercial and industrial space but also for homes, house lots, and garages. Fueled in part by highway access and government subsidies of home mortgages, households are building bigger homes and going further afield, finding cheaper land and plenty of open space. Space used for single-family homes has grown 44 percent between 1970 and 1998.[4] Yet the number of people per household declined by 17 percent during the same period.[5] In less urbanized areas of the country, the median size lot of a newly constructed home is over two times the size of lots for all homes.[6] The average acreage per house in rural towns in Rhode Island grew by 33 percent between the 1960s and the 1990s.[7]

Even garages have grown. Early detached garages were about 10 feet by 18 feet, enough for one car. Today's attached garages have room for at least two or three cars and space at the back for all the outdoor equipment of contemporary life. This has made a tremendous contribution to the growth in the size of the average home.

These images show the extension of one residential area from a neighborhood of inviting homes nestled along a common space—sidewalk, tree belt, and street (**Fig. 7.6**)—to an abandoned farm field where homes are spaced far apart (**Fig. 7.7**). In the older neighborhood, the dominant view is of the house's front steps and front door, which draw the visitor in. In **Fig. 7.7**, your eye is first drawn to the driveway and then to the garage. The front door—wherever it is—is only a formality, not an invitation. Instead of the street unifying the neighborhood, it keeps the houses apart.

The size of the buildings and lots determines whether the home will be

7.10 The neighborhoods of St. Albans City (top) and St. Albans Town (bottom).

an integral part of the neighborhood or an island marooned in a sea of grass. When we look behind the visual images of these two places, we can measure differences in the space that they occupy. In the older neighborhood, lot sizes average 13,500 square feet (**Fig. 7.8**, page 153). The lot sizes in the new neighborhood are two to three times those of the old neighborhood (**Fig. 7.9**, page 153). Streets are wider, too: 32 feet in the new neighborhood versus 22 feet in the older one. The lot sizes and setbacks in the newer neighborhood exceed the town zoning requirements. Clearly, the developer was offering what he thought the market would want by building above the town's minimum standards. The "market," it seems, preferred more detached retreats.

While these dimensional differences between the two neighborhoods may not seem large, they add up to a significant contrast in the use of space. If the dimensions of the older neighborhood had been applied to the new neighborhood, twice as many people could live there. That would mean more people sharing the common street and the invisible underground systems. Greater efficiency in the use of public services yields greater savings in public costs. If the older layout had been followed, not only would more space be available for additional housing (or, alternatively, community open space), but there would be more public savings (**Fig. 7.10**).

Many of the same people who are looking for large homes and lots in the countryside are also concerned with traffic congestion, clean air, rising property taxes and preserving open space. But they are often unaware that a greater number of large lots in the countryside will result in more congestion, less open space and clean air, and higher property taxes.

7.11 Homeowners seeking large lots may want to keep neighbors at a distance.

7.12 An enormous single-family house sits in seclusion in the woods.

THE COSTS OF SPRAWL

Consumers' and developers' interests in large lots are obvious in **Fig. 7.11**. Once again, the homes are sited at the greatest distance possible from the road and other homes. The desire for detachment is carried to the extreme by the enormous single-family home sitting alone in the woods (**Fig. 7.12**). It appears that the owners are making up for their isolation by placing everything they could possibly need under one roof. With more resources, people will push the scale of their lots and houses to greater extents. Yet the impact of the choices made by these homeowners can be costly to communities.

One way to measure the costs of spread out development is to compare how many miles of road are needed to serve development in suburban and rural communities versus urban centers. Three to four times more miles of road per 1,000 people are needed in suburban communities and about 10 times more in rural communities than in urban centers, according to a Chittenden County study.[8]

More roads mean higher costs. According to a 1998 national survey of studies on the impacts of sprawl, several authors have found that compact growth can save from 12 percent to 20 percent in road costs and from seven percent to14 percent in utility costs.[9] Other authors have found a 60 percent savings in road costs and 40 percent savings in utility costs in planned developments as opposed to sprawl developments.[10]

Despite the benefits of smaller lots, in many rural areas the lots are growing larger. The average new village lot in some Vermont towns is three to six times larger than traditional village lots. In these same towns, new households use an average of eight acres for a single-family home.[11]

In one community, the size of subdivided lots grew from 6,500 square feet in 1939 to over 300,000 square feet in 1972—a nearly 50-fold increase![12]

Larger lot sizes require longer sewer, water, and utility lines and more roads. The installation, operation, and maintenance costs of this infrastructure are often shared by the entire community, including those people living in nearby town centers. While fees assessed on developers help to defray some of the capital costs of these services, they do not cover all operating and maintenance costs. As a result, some residents living in compact neighborhoods end up helping to pay the bill for sprawl.

Often it is the rules established by rural towns that encourage large lots and the spread of housing into the countryside. **Figure 7.13** shows a real life example of excessive setback requirements: houses set back 60 feet from the street, forcing deep front yards and shortening rear ones. To satisfy the regulations and still provide home buyers with the spacious, private back yards they desire, a larger lot becomes necessary. The 30-foot-wide street required by the town's subdivision regulations adds to the volume of land consumed. The more this pattern is extended, the more land is broken into less useful pieces. The houses occupying a former farm in **Fig. 7.14** could have been arranged more compactly to leave a portion of the land open. But if local regulations dictate large lots and big setbacks, this is not possible.

7.13 Buildings here are set back 60 feet from the street to meet requirements in St. Albans Town.

7.14 Another view of the subdivision in Fig. 7.13. When the rules are applied to several streets, the spreading effect is multiplied.

7.15 Houses in this development appeal to only one market: people seeking single-family detached houses.

SUPPLY OR DEMAND?

Are these large lots what people want or are they just what's available? National Association of Homebuilders' data indicate that people will be looking for even larger single-family detached homes in the future.[13] But is everyone looking for the same thing? Apparently not, given growing evidence from around the country. According to *Builder* magazine, "Since most builders build homes in suburbia, they tend to be focused on families—the demographic group most likely to live in big houses on big lots. But so-called greenfield development has left many builders with a skewed image of the real demographic composition of our country."[14] U.S. Census data show that only 25 percent of households have children under the age of 18.[15] Who is providing for the needs of the elderly, single persons, low-income families, and empty nesters who are part of the remaining 75 percent of households (**Fig. 7.15**)?

Surveys illustrate that the market for housing is diverse. The Vermont Forum on Sprawl in 2000 found that 31 percent of respondents to a statewide poll preferred to live on a smaller lot in an urban or village center where they could walk to shops and services as opposed to a larger lot in the countryside where driving would be required for all trips.[16] In 1999 the Maine State Planning Office found that 37 percent of the total homebuyers' market can be considered "good targets for traditional neighborhood development,"[17] which by definition would have smaller lots than most other developments. The Concord Group of Newport Beach, California, has identified 14 different consumer groups with different wants and needs for housing.[18]

Nevertheless, homes and house lots are getting bigger. Survey after survey from rural parts of the country show that people who move to large lots in outlying areas are attempting to escape noise and traffic and to provide green space and privacy for their families. Unlike residents of more urbanized parts of the country, these people are not necessarily leaving because of poor schools or crime. They are fleeing higher density and all the problems they associate with more houses in less space. Yet some people in small towns with higher density settings have found privacy, quiet, safety, and beauty. If we are to take advantage of the potential market for infill housing in town centers and for new, compact neighborhoods, we must build with those needs in mind.

BIGGER ROADS

With bigger stores, bigger industrial buildings, bigger homes, and bigger lots, it is not surprising that we have bigger roads as well. As noted in Chapter 8, speed and accessibility are two important ingredients for meeting the needs of car and driver. As **Figs. 7.16 and 7.17** demonstrate, these two needs are sometimes taken to extremes in the design of neighborhood streets.

In **Fig. 7.16**, it is hard to tell which road is designed for more traffic and higher speeds, the dead end cul-de-sac or the state highway it connects to. Often towns require wide roads, gentle curves, and generous turning radii for all streets regardless of their use or traffic volume. These excessive designs encourage higher speeds and create a stark streetscape compared to narrow streets in similar low-traffic settings.

Another cul-de-sac, shown in **Fig. 7.17**, punctuates the landscape with its wide, curvy black-topped surface lined with gleaming white shoulders. The wide road terminates in a paved cul-de-sac 100 feet in diameter. It is unclear why a narrow street wouldn't do instead. The enormous cul-de-sac is the result of the local fire chief's demand for adequate space for turning fire trucks and his prohibition of islands that might otherwise soften the appearance.

A more traditional approach to neighborhood streets is illustrated in **Fig. 7.18**. The road is 20 feet wide, enough space for two cars to pass slowly and for occasional on-street parking. The road is designed for access, not for speed, and its narrowness helps to slow traffic.

Neighborhood streets not only provide for the occasional emergency vehicle but for the everyday safety of pedestrians and the quality of life of residents. Town planners today must juggle the desires for smaller streets with the demands for generous road standards made by street departments, fire chiefs, and rescue squads. Perhaps towns should reexamine how narrow village and city streets have been served by plows, fire trucks, and ambulances without harm to their inhabitants over the years.

7.17 A broad cul-de-sac pro-vides access to a few large rural houses.

7.16 A cul-de-sac serving a small subdivision is bigger than the state highway it connects to.

7.18 (below) A narrow street serving a compact neighborhood.

SMALLER SPACES, BETTER PLACES

How can we return to more compact forms of development in our rural towns? Retailers today cater to the needs of a broad region, not just those of the community where they are located. Growing industries seek spaces with long, flat layouts to meet contemporary production methods. Home owners go further and further from the edge of settled areas looking for a large piece of the countryside at a reasonable price. Town planning standards call for large lots, low lot coverage, wide roads, and low densities.

Communities, their residents, developers, and business owners need to find the answers to this question by taking a close look at their place within a larger region, the ability of their town centers to absorb more growth, the quality of their residential neighborhoods, and the regulations that the town uses to shape development.

MEETING COMMERCIAL NEEDS

Rutland City, Vermont, was once the retail center of Rutland County (**Fig. 7.19**). Its downtown included department stores, clothing stores, grocery stores, and others serving a wide range of community needs. As strip malls and shopping centers looked for roomier places in the next town, the city's role as a retail hub began to decline. In an effort to combat downtown vacancies, the city embarked on a downtown revitalization program. Slowly, through planning, public investment, and with the help of a broad coalition of residents, business people, and property owners, the city began to turn the downtown around. One dramatic indicator of its success was the decision by Wal-Mart to locate downtown, an unusual choice by the nation's largest retailer (**Fig. 7.20**). The 75,000-square-foot store was located in a rehabilitated shopping center on the old railroad yards directly across the street from the historic business district. Once again, the old regional center was able to attract a large regional retailer to its center.

By defining their role in the region, towns can make a realistic assessment of the market they can serve with new commercial development. Regional centers will serve a broad market. Their stores will be larger and offer a broader selection of goods. The challenge in these communities will be to find the space in or adjacent to town centers, as Rutland City did, to provide for the region's commercial needs, and to establish the regulations that regional retail development will have to meet.

Cities have the power to set the standards to which these national retailers must conform. A long, flat box was not going to work for the Burlington, Vermont, when a Filene's department store was proposed

7.19 *Rutland, Vermont, is working to revitalize its downtown.*

7.20 *A 75,000-square-foot Wal-Mart store in downtown Rutland.*

downtown (**Fig. 7.21**, page 164). Although there was room in the central business district for a one-story, 150,000-square-foot store, a two-story building was proposed to make a more compact retailing area. In an attempt to enhance the pedestrian environment, the city mandated that store windows line the first floor along the street. An unusually small, multi-story parking garage was built next door. The store required fewer parking spaces than suburban malls because at least 25 percent of the shopping trips would be by foot, bicycle, or transit. Shared parking opportunities at other sites in the city also reduced the parking required under the city's zoning ordinance

These two examples illustrate how large, regional retail stores can fit within town centers if designed carefully. In both cases, however, the communities had to make huge efforts to lure the retailers to their sites. It took ingenuity, public money, and community commitment to offset the advantages that most retailers find in the fields outside of town.

Smaller communities need not accommodate large regional retailers. In these towns, commerce can be scaled down to meet the needs of local residents. Some communities have insured an appropriate scale by establishing limits on the size of commercial buildings and uses. To make new buildings attractive to pedestrians and compatible with the traditional character of town centers, communities have also required that buildings adjoin public sidewalks and meet streetscape design standards for street trees, sidewalks, lighting, benches, and underground utilities. These amenities help to make the area attractive to first floor commercial tenants

7.21 *A new Filene's department store with adjacent decked parking in downtown Burlington, Vermont.*

and apartment dwellers upstairs.

Before deciding that more commercial space is needed outside the town center, communities should examine the potential for filling in within the town center. In the small city of Vergennes, Vermont, over 135,000 square feet of underused land and buildings were found within the downtown through a survey of property records and on site inspection[19] (**Fig. 7.22**).

If there is not enough space to handle projected growth in the town center, communities can take steps to minimize the amount of land consumed in peripheral areas by commerce or industry. If greater lot coverages, small lots, and reduced setbacks are permitted, new compact business centers may be established.

7.22 *Infill development on these sites in downtown Vergennes, Vermont, could substantially increase commercial space.*

7.23 In Waterbury, Vermont, a neighborhood provides privacy, safety, green space, and low traffic volumes while taking up a relatively small amount of land.

SMALL LOT HOUSING WITH BIG LOT AMENITIES

Many people like the idea of living near their jobs, shops, the post office, or their children's schools, but they may assume these neighborhoods are crowded or noisy. They may believe the small back yards offer no privacy. In many small towns there may be some merit to these perceptions. Through traffic may be allowed to speed on residential streets. Local streets, sidewalks, and tree belts may not be maintained, giving the neighborhood a forlorn appearance. Yet, with careful design and upkeep, these neighborhoods can offer a desirable alternative to large lots in the countryside.

The village neighborhood in **Fig. 7.23** is a residential area that provides privacy, low traffic, safety, and green space while using only a small amount of land. Although the houses are located close together and directly on the street, each home has a private backyard separated from its neighbors by plantings and garages. The street is narrow, offering just enough space for two cars to pass each other. The narrow width helps to slow traffic. Children can safely play in these yards or ride their bicycles on the sidewalks.

The housing in this village is mixed. Not every house is for a single family. Apartments are provided in old carriage houses and in additions onto the backs of homes. Density has been added to this neighborhood without detracting from its overall character. Communities can build this flexibility into their development regulations by allowing accessory apartments in single-family areas, permitting the adaptive reuse of outbuildings, such as carriage houses and barns, for apartments, or allowing a

7.24 New houses in Stowe, Vermont, are close to the street on small lots, but offer plenty of backyard decks, lawns, and gardens.

duplex on the same size lot as a single-family residence.

There are other ways to increase the number of housing units per acre while keeping the perception that the area is low density. One survey showed that residents are as satisfied with six or seven units per acre as they are with three or four.[20] Factors that contribute to the perception of lower density are the presence of open space, low building heights, landscaping, short blocks, and small groups of housing.[21] A high-quality design can make higher density units attractive. A very successful project in Stowe, Vermont, bucked local trends by offering homes on small lots along a narrow drive. The small front yards left plenty of space out back for decks, lawns, and gardens (**Fig. 7.24**, page 165).

COMMUNITY-MINDED REGULATIONS

Communities possess perhaps the most powerful tool of all to address the scale of development: local zoning regulations. We have seen how these regulations can spread out development and cause overly consumptive land use patterns. Likewise, zoning can do the opposite. It can tighten up development, intensify it, and make it more efficient and attractive (**Fig. 7.25**).

Zoning provisions can require commercial and industrial development to use up a larger area of a lot, to fit onto a smaller lot, to build up to the street, and to share parking with neighboring properties. Multi-story structures can be mandated in order to use land and public services, such as roads, water, and sewer, more efficiently.

Zoning provisions can lead to a more flexible approach to housing in residential neighborhoods and town centers. By diversifying the types of housing permitted, zoning can increase density without changing the appearance of an area. Amenities such as street trees and small parks can be required in order to add to neighborhood appeal. Encouraging developers to build close to the street and put garages out back can help to provide privacy behind homes. Narrowing the streets to calm traffic helps reduce noise and safety problems.

With communities offering higher density opportunities through progressive regulations, developers choosing designs that take advantage of new regulations, and residents and businesses choosing a more community conscious lifestyle, we can reduce the scale of development in our rural towns. The result will be better use of limited resources, including public utilities and open land, and a community-minded pattern of development.

7.25 *A village in Peacham, Vermont, retains its small scale and offers a diversity of housing.*

NOTES

1. Natural Resources Conservation Service, U.S. Department of Agriculture. Natural Resources Inventory, 1997. Also: U.S. Bureau of the Census. U.S. Census of Population, 1982 and 1997. Both sets of data exclude Alaska.

2. Vermont Forum on Sprawl. *Exploring Sprawl #5: The Costs of Development: Downtowns vs. Open Space,* Burlington, Vermont, 1999.

3. This is due to large setbacks, small lot coverages, and parking and open space standards that limit the space a building can use. By contrast, setbacks in downtowns are small or nonexistent, lot coverages are high, parking is met off site or underground, and open space is limited to tree belts and nearby parks.

4. The median size of a new home was 1,385 square feet in 1970. By 1998, the median size had increased to 2,000 square feet. U.S. Bureau of the Census and U.S. Department of Housing and Urban Development, *Current Construction Reports,* Series C-25, *Characteristics of New Housing,* 1998.

5. U.S. Statistical Abstract, 1999, Population, Table 70.

6. Outside of metropolitan areas, the median lot size for all single-family detached housing units is .70 acres. For newly built single-family housing units, the median lot size is 1.56 acres. The median lot size for all single-family housing units is .35 acres. U.S. Census Bureau, *Current Housing Reports,* Series H150/97, *American Housing Survey of the United States,* 1997.

7. HCPC, Inc. and Planimetrics, LLP, *The Costs of Suburban Sprawl and Urban Decay in Rhode Island,* Smart Growth Rhode Island, Providence, December 1999, p. 5.

8. Miles of road per 1,000 residents in 1995: in urban centers, 2.7 miles; in suburban towns, 9.3 miles; in rural towns, 21.4 miles; all, 8 miles. Source: Champlain Initiative. *The History of Sprawl in Chittenden County,* Burlington, Vermont, March 1999, p. 14.

9. Robert W. Burchell, et al. *The Costs of Sprawl Revisited,* Transportation Research Board, Washington, D.C. 1998, p. 137.

10. Ibid., p. 138.

11. Champlain Initiative, p. 27.

12. Ibid., p. 17.

13. National Association of Home Builders, *Housing at the Millennium, Facts, Figures and Trends, 1900, 1950, 2000,* Washington, D.C., 2000, p. 4.

14. "How Big Is the Market?" *Builder,* July 1998, p. 114.

15. Ibid., p. 114.

16. Vermont Forum on Sprawl and Center for Rural Studies, *Vermonter Poll 2000,* University of Vermont, 2000.

17. Maine State Planning Office, *Market for Traditional Neighborhoods,* Augusta, Maine, August 1999, p. 5.

18. Marcia Mogelonsky. "Reconfiguring the American Dream," *American Demographics,* January 1997, p. 2.

19. University of Vermont Historic Preservation Students for Vermont Forum on Sprawl. *Finding Space Downtown,* Burlington, Vermont, April 2000.

20. Reid Ewing and Robert Hodder, *Best Development Practices: A Primer for Smart Growth,* Smart Growth Network, p. 27.

21. Ibid., p. 27.

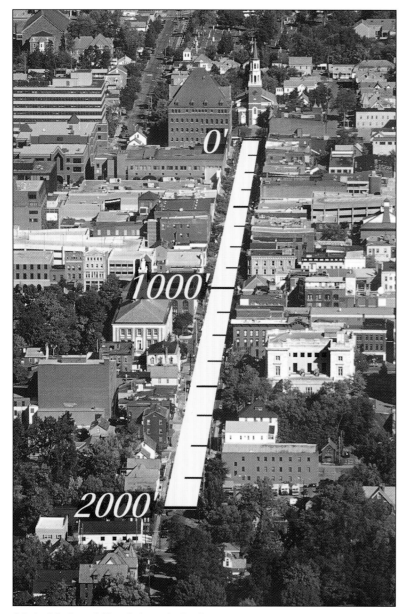

8.2 *Aerial view of Church Street in Burlington, Vermont.*

8.3 *Aerial view of Tafts Corners in Williston.*

late a minimum number of parking spaces (**Fig. 8.8**). The underlying assumption in many of the formulas is that everyone will arrive by car, and that they will occupy a space while visiting that one business and then drive on to their next destination. As a result, each new store, restaurant, or office building must have its own lot serving only its own customers. And when the ratio is calculated, each building sits next to a pad of asphalt as big as, if not bigger than, the building itself.

The commercial district in **Fig. 8.9** was built according to this formula, and it illustrates how a common set of decisions can perpetuate auto-oriented sprawl.

The first decision was about location. The developer of these retail buildings, together with the national retail chains planning to occupy them, chose to locate at an interstate interchange rather than close to existing population centers. They also chose a site not served by public transportation. Unless the community subsidized an expansion of the regional bus service, the car would be the sole means of travel for store patrons. And since walking, biking, or taking the bus to this area was not an option, the buildings would need enough parking spaces to accommodate every visitor.

A second decision was to build large stores. This ratcheted up the number of spaces per building. And rather than share parking lots, each building was provided with its own lot, increasing the distance between stores.

The final decision that destined this place to remain auto-dependent was the design and arrangement of buildings. The developer built side-

8.9 Built for cars, not people. This shopping area in Williston, Vermont, is remote from other destinations, its buildings are too far apart for comfortable walking, and its lots are huge and inhospitable, as shown in Fig. 8.10.

walks and crosswalks, but the layout of the site prevents the place from attracting many people on foot. The scale of the site, the distance between buildings, the vast parking lots to cross, and circuitous connections eliminate any incentive for people to travel from store to store on foot. **Figure 8.10** shows the view from the exit of one store to the front door of another one "across the street." Imagine being there and wanting to get to that distant doorway. Would you follow the quarter mile of sidewalk on its roundabout course? Would you strike out across the parking lot and scramble through the landscaping? Or would you get back in your car and drive over there? Without a comfortable pedestrian environment, this shopping center will continue to be auto-dependent, even as the land around it gets developed and it becomes less isolated.

This pattern represents the extreme to which we've shaped our towns to fit the proportion of the automobile. At the urban edge, where green fields lie waiting, there are no older buildings to remind us of the human scale. There is only space, ready for paving. Couple this with an attitude that the car is our only acceptable way of getting around, and places like this are bound to emerge.

In new growth areas, the space requirements of the automobile can be met without restriction, but what happens when the one-car-per-visitor formula is applied to villages and downtowns?

In areas that are already settled, it is not simply a matter of claiming open land for parking areas. They must be carved out of the existing urban fabric. This often means replacing buildings or yards with asphalt.

And when the parking lot is placed in front, as retailers often prefer, several buildings must be removed. A gap appears on Main Street, and the traditional pattern of streets and buildings is disrupted (**Fig. 8.11**). It becomes a little less comfortable to walk along, a little less appealing to be in. But the effect is not just aesthetic. Space that had been used for human activity is replaced by space used to store cars. As more parking spaces are claimed, the density of Main Street is lowered and the number of services it offers declines.

8.10

8.11 When the one-car-per-customer parking formula is applied to villages where the land is already spoken for, buildings get demolished and the traditional pattern of Main Street is disrupted. That is what happened in Enosburg, Vermont.

Since the middle of the 20th century, when the number of car owners increased dramatically, towns across the country have faced the issue of downtown parking. They have responded differently to the problem of providing space for the car, with attitudes changing over the decades. During the urban renewal era, many towns razed whole blocks to free up space for parking lots. In later years, communities took less disruptive actions like building garages or consolidating rear yards to create municipal parking lots. Some towns continue to make their downtowns more car-friendly, becoming more suburban in order to compete with the suburbs. Others struggle to strike a balance between gridlock and suburbanization. They have come to realize that given the scale of the car, there is simply not enough space available in urban settings to cater exclusively to the car and still retain a downtown. As space is designed and redesigned for cars instead of people, the character of our communities changes.[1]

SPEED

Speed is the other factor that has changed the face of our landscape. In the past century, as the speed of our movement has increased, we have spread out more and cared about the quality of our surroundings less.

The generations that came before us, who built our downtowns and villages, perceived space at the scale of the human body and designed places that would fit its speed and range. The fact that walking was the prime mode of transportation had a profound effect on the form of towns. Commercial development was contained within a certain walking distance. The use of land was optimized. But now that we are firmly entrenched in the automobile age, the constraint that shaped compact towns is gone. We have a very different sense of scale based on the speed of the automobile.

The faster a vehicle moves, the more space it needs to maneuver and the bigger its impact on its immediate surroundings. At higher speeds, motorists take in a scene on a more superficial level, missing the details of a place that are important to the pedestrian. The suburban intersection shown earlier (**Fig. 8.3**, see page 172) is a place designed for greater speed. It can be comprehended on a gross level, when the spaces between the buildings are shrunk by the speed of a car, but it's an environment that doesn't offer much complexity or richness to those traveling more slowly.

Consider the differences between a place where traffic moves at 20 miles per hour and one in which it moves at 40. At 20 mph, roads can be narrow and signs can be small. When traffic moves slowly, a driver has more time to take in his surroundings, to see pedestrians or other obsta-

8.12 Interchanges at interstate highways require a lot of space because they are designed for the smooth flow of vehicles. In Norwich, Vermont, the interchange takes up more room than the small village it connects to.

cles. But at 40 mph, he has less time to see and to stop. Highway signs must be larger. Turns are broader and more sweeping, and lanes are wider. There can be no buildings or trees infringing on a motorist's view of approaching traffic. The higher the speed, the less there can be in the immediate area (**Fig. 8.13**, page 182). Places designed for fast-moving cars are often sterile environments that allocate vast spaces to a single use. The interstate interchange shown in **Fig. 8.12** is larger than the neighboring village of 870 residents. Wide shoulders, turning lanes, and large turning radii allow vehicles to move quickly, but at the cost of substantial land. In fact, construction of this interchange forced the removal of a second village that had been clustered around the original road. The earlier road was narrow and winding with buildings on either side, an environment that was full of human activity but not conducive to quick traffic flow.

The infrastructure of speed, perfected with the interstate highway system, has been transplanted by bits and pieces into some downtowns and villages. Where space is tight, vehicles gain speed as pedestrians lose ground. Rights-of-way are limited, so when lanes are widened and corners are carved away, there is less room for green belts and sidewalks. Traffic signals are timed to keep the cars moving, but pedestrians are stalled at the corners waiting to cross. These communities have widened their streets, eliminated two-way traffic, removed on-street parking, or added over-scaled signs. The effect is to create a central business district that is easy to pass through but unlikely to tempt a driver to stop and explore.

Many small villages located on major highways have felt the impact of

8.13 *In places where everyone travels at 40 mph, the inevitable result is a wide-open, horizontal landscape of highway development, as in Essex, Vermont.*

this obsession with traffic flow. Their Main Streets, which also happen to be the through route for an increasing number of cars and trucks, have been radically altered by highway "improvement" projects. **Figure 8.14** shows one village whose Main Street was engineered for speed in a recent state highway department road project. The street through the village was widened and straightened, and on-street parking was eliminated. The visual message for passing motorists is "step on it."

8.14 *When the main street in a small town is also part of a state road, the need for speed may take precedence over local values. This recently reengineered street in South Hero, Vermont, is an example*

8.15 *A rural intersection in South Burlington, Vermont, circa 1937. The relatively few drivers included long-distance travelers, Sunday drivers, and farmers going to market. Source: Courtesy of Burlington Public Works.*

KEEPING THE CAR IN PERSPECTIVE

In their book, *Where the Sky and the Road Collide*, Kevin and Todd Berger, two self-proclaimed "car biologists," set out to study the complex ecosystem of driving. The car, they claimed, is endangered by its own overpopulation. They cite overcrowded highways, environmental degradation, and the drain on economic resources as some of the forces threatening the car's habitat.[2]

In many ways, rural areas are the perfect car habitat. They have miles of open road and plenty of space for storage. Driving on a country road, we can take in the scenery, enjoy the thrill of speed, and be perfectly comfortable. Because cars are few in number, there is little competition for space on the road, no reason to slow or stop. And when we choose to stop, we know there will be a free parking space.

This is the experience that rural dwellers are accustomed to, and naturally, they would be reluctant to let go of it. They have the best of both worlds: the benefits of the car, without its negative impacts. In rural areas, the car is accommodated but the landscape is intact. There are no traffic lights, parking lots are small, and the landscape is a constant and enveloping presence.

In growing towns, this rural idyll eventually succumbs to a more suburban reality. Over time, many more people and many more cars arrive. Wherever they come together—to work, to shop, to socialize—their greater numbers destroy the perfect driving habitat, clogging roads and vying for parking. So fields give way to large parking lots and wide roads as the rural landscape is altered to provide space and maintain speed for the cars. This change is illustrated in **Figs. 8.15 and 8.16**.

8.16 *By 1999, the country road had turned into a six-lane highway serving commuters and shoppers as well as travelers.*

As rural towns grow, they face a major decision. One choice is to hold fast to their very close relationship with the automobile: assuming that all trips will be made in the car, which will move quickly and be parked near the door. They will subdivide land, lay out sites, and build structures with a driver's sense of scale. They will create 40 mph places, which will look and function like a highway strip or edge city.

Or they can imagine a different relationship with the car and create a different settlement pattern, one in which the automobile is just *one* of several ways to get around. The places where people want to go are close together. They can be reached easily and conveniently on foot. With this alternative approach the automobile doesn't dictate the form of a place but is a guest in an environment designed for the scale and pace of the human body. These 20 mph places have more shops, offices, schools, and homes than could fit in places designed solely for the car. Like the traditional small towns they are modeled on, they offer many choices within a small area.

Small local governments can't unilaterally shift from car dependency to a more balanced transportation system. Without regional cooperation and investment, train and bus service is not an option. But they do have the power to create towns that will make alternatives possible. They can channel growth into their existing center, whether it is a full-fledged downtown or a crossroads hamlet. Although they don't control regional transportation funding decisions, they can control the land use pattern in their town. And, as most transportation planners understand by now, land use is destiny. A compact center where people live, shop, and work offers the bright-

est transportation future. With fewer residents living out in the country, there will be fewer commuters overloading the existing road network. More residents in the center will provide the critical mass necessary to make regional transit feasible. And with a greater density and diversity of uses in the village, people will be less dependent on their cars to get where they need to go. By growing in a traditional compact pattern, small towns can provide their residents with the cheapest and most basic transportation option: walking.

The key to creating a 20 mph place lies in thinking like a pedestrian, not a driver. Whether the project is the construction of a single building or a plan for a whole new part of town, mentally removing ourselves from the car is the first step. When we do that, scale shrinks and public space matters. We are forced to think about the type of detail that is necessary to make a beautiful place.

8.17-8.18 *These cars are parked on the top level of a two-story structure in the middle of a downtown block. There are 30 cars parked below and more in a parking lot on the adjacent site.*

FITTING IN

The better land use practices described in earlier chapters can help us need the car less, but chances are, we'll still want it around. How can we accommodate it without letting it take over? Cars demand a certain amount of space, but we can be a lot more ingenious about how we store and move them. The architect Daniel Soloman, who has designed several apartment buildings for downtown San Francisco, has found that cars are "much more malleable than the one dimensional pragmatism of most traffic engineers suggests. They fit into all kinds of places, they maneuver, they park, even in the most ancient and beautiful cities." He urges designers to alter the standard building-parking formula to help tame the car and "make it into an innocuous object of service, not the dominant feature of urban life."[3] His projects illustrate how cars can be tucked under and behind buildings, and how to use courtyards and service alleys to create spaces where cars and people can peacefully coexist.

When we think about storing cars we usually imagine a single parking lot next to a single building. This image has become so deeply ingrained in the minds of drivers and builders in the past 50 years that for many people, especially those in rural towns, it's hard to imagine anything else. The alternative, however, is alive and well in many small American cities that were built before the motor age but retrofitted for the car. Wherever space is at a premium, we tend to be careful about how we use it. In older cities, parking spaces are tucked into side alleys, or carved out of basements or inner block service areas. They're placed along streets, stacked in parking garages, and slipped under houses.

8.18

8.19 There was little need for parking in Burlington in 1937. Off-street paved areas are shown in red.

8.20 To accommodate cars downtown, the city of Burlington allowed on-street parking, built multi-level garages, and encouraged shared parking. Many of the lots (in red) and parking garages (in purple) are located behind, above, or under buildings. The lots are small and dispersed.

Burlington, Vermont, had few parking lots in 1937 (**Fig. 8.19**). There wasn't much need for them back then. But as the number of drivers living and working in the city has increased, parking spaces have multiplied. As the years passed, if Burlington officials had applied the parking-lot-per-building approach, there wouldn't have been much city left by 1995. Instead, the city allowed on-street parking, built multi-level garages, and encouraged shared parking in the middle of city blocks (**Fig. 8.20**). Drivers can leave their cars on the street, in a lot (shown in red) or in a garage (shown in purple). The lots and garages are dispersed and small in scale. Many are behind or under buildings (**Figs. 8.17** and **8.18**, page 185). Despite the addition of almost 4,000 parking spaces over the course of 60 years, the pattern of the city has not been overwhelmed by the car. Downtown Burlington remains a safe and comfortable place for pedestrians and bicyclists. And the city's compact pattern makes it possible for transportation alternatives to work, such as a park-and-ride shuttle, a regional bus service, and a commuter train.

Contrast Burlington's pattern with an auto-oriented one. **Figure 8.21** (page 188) shows a place where a concern for the turning movements and storage requirements of the automobile got out of hand. Buildings are randomly sited along the highway, and parking lots seep from parcel to parcel. There are many more square feet of asphalt (shown in yellow) than are needed to serve the number of drivers using the space. The large amount of paved land makes it possible to turn and park almost anywhere, indulging the driver's slightest whims. It's easy to drive there, but ugly to look at. Anyone seen walking there would inspire pity. Car broke down?

Can't afford one? Only the desperate enter this place on foot.

Figure 8.22 (page 188) shows a pattern that allows both pedestrians *and* drivers an opportunity to get around. This illustrates the typical mid-block parking scenario common in traditional downtowns. Buildings are lined up on the sidewalk. Parking is available in lots in the interior of the block as well as on the street. There are connections between the street and the inner block through alleys and driveways as well as through the buildings. Several businesses share the parking lots. Spaces used during the day are vacated for others to occupy at night. Are there enough spaces within the block for every customer at every hour of the day? Probably not. But there is additional parking on the streets or in the public garages nearby. Some may have a longer walk to the door, but people are usually willing to walk farther distances in a pleasant environment.

The paved areas (also shown in yellow) are tightly confined and are limited to the essential number needed to serve the surrounding buildings. Trees within the block and along the street further reduce the scale of the parking areas by creating an overhead canopy. Although cars can operate here, the size and movement of vehicles have not dictated the form of this place.

Following the urban parking model (**Fig. 8.22**, page 188) rather than the contemporary pattern (**Fig. 8.21**, page 188), small towns growing into larger towns can have it both ways. If they plan their communities to follow a compact pattern, they can accommodate cars but still create a place that's worth being in.

8.21 *A highway outside Hardwick, Vermont, where concern for the turning movements and storage requirements of cars got out of hand. Paved areas are in yellow.*

8.22 *In downtown Burlington, parking is available in the center of the block and along the streets, allowing both drivers and pedestrians to get around rather easily.*

PARK AND WALK

Figures 8.23 to 8.30 (pages 189-191) show how, over time, Manchester, Vermont, experienced a shift in its thinking about the automobile. The aerial photograph taken in 1995 (**Fig. 8.24**, page 190) shows about a mile of highway running through town, with three different patterns visible. At the bottom is the pre-automobile era pattern of Main Street. The buildings, built before cars came on the scene, are placed within a tight cluster along the street, which was designed for the comfort and convenience of people travelling its length on foot. It was unnecessary and undesirable for the buildings to be separated and for the entrances to be far from the sidewalk. Without cars, people had limited range of movement. There was a real incentive to make the most of available space.

The pattern shown at the top reveals a different approach toward organizing space. It was laid out at a time when Manchester had accepted the notion that travel by car was preferable to walking. There was no pressing need to place the buildings close together, nor was there even a reason to connect them with sidewalks. It was assumed that every visitor to these buildings would arrive by car.

The middle area shows a transition period between the pedestrian pattern of the 19th century and the auto pattern of the post war years. Originally designed as a neighborhood of single-family homes, these buildings were set back from the street to provide space for front yards. As the business district expanded and the homes were converted to shops, the space around the buildings was also altered to make room for parked cars. Many of the front yards were converted to parking lots. As a result,

8.23 A new "park and walk" sign in Manchester, Vermont, directs drivers to leave their cars in one spot and tour the village on foot.

8.24

this segment of the corridor has a traditional building pattern, but a contemporary parking and circulation pattern.

Manchester draws tourists and shoppers from a broad region, and the number of visitors has grown rapidly, frequently overwhelming the village. The conventional engineering solution to the presence of more cars would be to widen roads and provide more parking lots to serve the increasing number of drivers. But by the mid-1990s, Manchester had again altered its thinking about the role of the automobile in a village setting. In the course of an earlier public planning process (described in Chapter 2), it had come to value the older, pre-automobile pattern. It now took an alternative approach to the congestion problem, getting shoppers out of their cars by improving the pedestrian environment. Called the "park and walk" strategy, the approach was to calm traffic and build safe and comfortable connections between buildings (**Fig. 8.23**, page 189).

Over the past five years, Manchester has managed to retrofit segment 3 by adding buildings on the street and narrowing intersections. It has also restored some of the greenery to segment 2 and added sidewalks. Its aim is to tie together shops from one end of the village to the other with sidewalks, lined with small-scale buildings and street trees. Visitors arrive in town, park their car in one of several parking lots, and tour the village on foot.

In changing the street environment, this community is striving to balance the needs of passersby, visitors, and residents. While it recognizes that cars are going to continue to dominate the transportation system, it has kept the needs of the automobile in perspective.

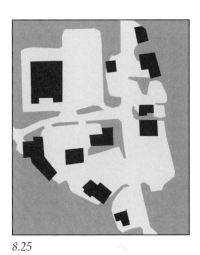

8.25

8.26

8.28

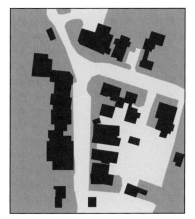

8.27

Opposite page: 8.24 Three different patterns are visible in this highway running through Manchester Center, Vermont.

8.25 and 8.26 A car-dependent pattern.

8.27 and 8.28 A transition pattern: As the business district expanded into this neighborhood and houses were converted to shops, the space around buildings was altered to make room for parked cars.

8.29 and 8.30 The Main Street pattern: Buildings are tightly clustered along the street, which was designed for the comfort of pedestrians.

8.29

8.30

DIVIDED LOYALTIES

If a rural area is the perfect car habitat, the emergence of sprawl in the countryside is diminishing our last, best driving opportunities. The Bergers suggest that we consider the car endangered and, tongue-in-cheek, propose a "save the car" movement. In their eyes, this is what it would take for auto-obsessed Americans to protect their own habitat.[4] Their idea is somewhat flip but worth considering as an appeal to reshape our environment. The key is to remake towns into places where driving is an act of occasional pleasure rather than a daily drudgery. Keeping within a traditional pattern and restoring public transportation would limit our need for the car, keeping the number of cars down and the roads uncrowded. In the process this strategy would also create a more sustainable and livable environment.

Through local planning efforts, many communities are striving to create places where pedestrians are comfortable and cars are not essential. Burlington has maintained its walkable pattern in the face of expanding parking demands. Manchester has worked hard to tie its growing village together with a pedestrian system. Communities can lessen their dependence on the car by planning for compact development and investing in the infrastructure that supports alternative transportation. But their efforts won't pay off unless individuals rethink their relationship with the car as well.

American adults average 72 minutes a day behind the wheel.[5] What do we hope for during that hour and 12 minutes? We want speed and continuous movement—to get to where we're going without slowing for another driver or stopping at a light. And above all, we want a parking place beside the door of the building we want to enter. Comfortably insulated and moving quickly, we rarely notice the details of the places we're driving through unless they slow us down. In the car, the rich environment of a village or downtown—buildings hugging the street, people and cyclists crossing our path, all the other lively details of an urban setting—is an annoyance because it impedes our movement.

These are the urges that developers of strip shopping centers and highway engineers satisfy so well. Wide roads, big signs, huge parking lots—many of the emblems of sprawl—are an attempt to make life easier for the driver in each of us. The more we drive, the more we want these automotive comforts. But as the first two images in this chapter illustrate, on foot we want something quite different. We need a diverse, comfortable, and beautiful environment to sustain us as pedestrians. The more we walk, the more we demand these qualities in our everyday surroundings.

This is how individuals affect the settlement pattern through their transportation choices. If you live out in the country, far from work, from school, and from all the other services you need on a daily basis, you are completely dependent on your car. This puts you in a driver's state of mind and makes it more likely that you will make choices about where to shop, work, and socialize based on how easy it is to drive to and park. You help to provide a market for strip development and interchange sprawl (**Fig. 8.32**). Developers locate video stores or supermarkets out on the highway not because they want to spoil rural scenery but because they

8.32 *The large parking lots, easy access, and high visibility of these businesses in Randolph, Vermont, appeal to the driver in us. From behind the wheel of a car, we are attracted to the convenience that these features offer.*

8.31 *The buildings hugging the street, intersecting the driveways, crosswalks, and parked cars of downtown Bellows Falls, Vermont, create a satisfying pedestrian experience, but the driver in us feels hassle and restricted movement.*

know that you will find it convenient to stop there on your drive home.

If you live in a city or village, close to the center, you are likely to make a different set of choices. You have the opportunity to get around on foot or bike, perhaps by bus. You seek out downtown businesses because they're convenient. With a greater array of services in a small area around your house, your range is smaller, so car trips are shorter. You don't need wide roads or big parking lots to make your daily life easy (**Fig. 8.31**, page 193).

As individuals, we choose where to live and how to travel, and, collectively, these choices affect the settlement pattern emerging in our communities. If we want a traditional pattern, we must make personal decisions to support that pattern. Living in town, carpooling, riding a bike, walking, taking the bus: These actions reinforce compact development because they lessen our dependence on the car, sprawl's great enabler.

CARS ARE US

The automobile has made all the contemporary patterns described in previous chapters possible. It has enabled us to pursue our desires for cheap land, for bucolic scenery, and for distance from whatever unpleasantness modern life has to offer.

Widespread use of the car accelerated the exodus from center to edge. It allowed us to line the roads out of town with stores, restaurants, and offices, and to subdivide the perimeter into larger and larger building sites. Although suburbs had emerged by the early 20th century, they were shaped by the constraints of walking, buses, trolleys, and trains. These transportation modes didn't generate the same dispersed pattern. Living on a field, miles from the nearest village, was a viable option only for those working the land. Nor was it viable to build a house in a wilderness area.

Cars have enabled us to spread our functions—working, shopping, playing—into separate areas of town and even distant corners of a region. Their speed has allowed us to widen the circle of our daily rounds from several blocks to several towns. We can put distance between groups of people. It is easier to set the local retirement home, the affordable housing project, or the high school off on its own than to weave it into the fabric of a neighborhood. Cars allow us to avoid each other.

Finally, the automobile has given us the opportunity to spread out and claim more space. The pre-motor-age, traditional pattern dictated that space be used efficiently and creatively, that house design maximize floor space, that buildings be arranged compactly within a lot, that privacy be created through careful design. This is apparent in Bristol, in Vergennes, in Barre, and in many of the other traditional downtowns and neighborhoods illustrated in earlier chapters. Cars freed us from these restrictions and allowed us to substitute acres of land for thoughtful design and planning.

NOTES

1. For a comprehensive examination of the car and its impacts on cities and towns, see Jane Holtz Kay's *Asphalt Nation: How the Automobile Took Over America and How We Can Take It Back.* New York, Crown Publishers, 1997.

2. K.T. Berger, *Where the Sky and the Road Collide: America Through the Eyes of its Drivers,* New York, Henry Holt, 1993, pp. 21-24.

3. Daniel Soloman. *Rebuilding,* New York, Princeton Architectural Press, 1992, p. 43.

4. Berger, pp. 21-24.

5. Robert B. Putnam. *Bowling Alone: The Collapse and Revival of American Community,* New York, Simon and Schuster, 2000, p. 212.

Look at the rural landscape from above and you will see our attitudes toward land revealed in the patterns on the ground. This book has illustrated two themes of contemporary development that spring from those attitudes. One is the spiral effect, our tendency to pursue a goal in an endless cycle of gratification and frustration. We leave our suburban neighborhood for a place in the country and 10 years later the country has vanished. Giving chase, we move again, farther out, only to see the elusive "rural character" fade away once more. What we want is an unspoiled rural landscape, but in pursuing it, what we get is sprawl. Our urge for one thing creates its opposite. So it is with roads. We want to drive from place to place with unrestricted ease. When there are too many cars on the road, we build a new highway. Within a few years, its lanes are clogged. Trying to recapture that lost sense of speed, we widen the road, and it fills again. The same holds true with private enclaves. Feeling the lack of security and beauty in our built environment, we try to escape to a place without problems, like a 10-acre lot or a gated community. Without our investment and support, the public realm degenerates. The worse it gets, the more we want to isolate ourselves, fortifying the enclave or escaping to somewhere else.

Like a dog chasing its tail, we pursue the dream of unlimited space, unrestricted movement, and total control. But if we get it, we can't hold it for long because everybody else wants it, too. This is another thread running through the book. As many individuals make the same choices—to live in the country on a big lot, to drive everywhere, to make buying decisions based on where it's easiest to drive and park—the impacts emerge with a certain mathematical inevitability. It seems that our bigger lifestyle decisions and the smaller personal choices we make every day are not in synch with what we want for our common future.

But this book also reveals another phenomenon. It highlights a growing trend among a few communities to realign their personal and collective land development goals in order to protect their future. This alternative pattern, also seen from above, reveals an attempt by residents of small towns and rural areas to look beyond their immediate, personal desires to a long-term public good.

The many examples of historic renovation, infill development, farmland preservation, community investment, and environmental protection featured in this book illustrate exactly how people can get beyond contemporary development practices to shape a landscape that serves future generations. Developers and governments are beginning to invest their resources in compact, walkable cities and villages that offer homes, jobs, goods, services, and a healthy community life to a wide range of people. They are taking steps to limit development on natural resource lands, such as farmland, wetlands, and forests. And a growing number of people are interested in living in town rather than out in the countryside.

This book has shown how individuals, acting alone or within organizations, have a hand in the fate of the rural landscape. If you would like to strengthen the emerging trend toward a more sustainable rural settlement pattern, you have many opportunities.

As an *individual*, you can help prevent sprawl through your larger lifestyle choices as well as in the small decisions you make every day. If you're contemplating moving, choose a home in an urban or village neighborhood, close to the places you need to visit. Density is your friend. It will give you more choices—for work, shopping, socializing, entertainment, and transportation—within a small area. If you already live in an urban neighborhood and it doesn't satisfy you, try to make it better by joining with your neighbors to reduce noise, slow traffic, or help improve the school. Recognize that *greater* density is not your enemy. If an infill development has been proposed for your neighborhood, welcome the possibility of new neighbors while carefully scrutinizing the project's design. Patronize downtown stores. Reward with your business the merchants who maintain historic village buildings, and support the economy and civic life of the community. Buy locally grown food to support the farmers who maintain the landscape you cherish. If you live in the country, consider donating a conservation easement to a land trust. Support the neighboring farmers' right to farm. Think about joining with neighbors to buy a crucial parcel of open land. If you are a farmer, consider selling the development rights to your property or reaching out to your neighbors by offering them special arrangements for a share of your produce. Get involved with local planning, form a citizens' planning group, or join the planning commission or conservation commission. Drafting a town plan and zoning ordinances is a public process. You have a right to participate, and if you want to protect the traditional settlement pattern of your community, you have a duty.

If you are already a *member of a local board*, such as a planning commission, that deals with development issues, you can make a difference in several ways. Imagine the future with a "build-out map" and use this for public discussion of a future growth plan. Take a long-term view of growth; plan an interconnected street network serving small lots and linking neighborhoods to village centers. Avoid strip zoning along highways. Involve citizens in researching the valuable natural resources in their communities and encourage them to work with experts to make recommendations for action in their town plans and local regulations. Establish a greenbelt of interconnected farmland or open space that is clearly defined and protected for the long term. Require a cluster development permit process in rural areas to protect agricultural, scenic, and wildlife habitat areas.

Work with adjoining communities to protect common resources, such as riparian corridors and wildlife habitats. Use land use regulations to require mixed uses, multi-story buildings, and mixed income housing. Encourage "courts" or quiet back streets that extend the local street network rather than isolated cul-de-sacs. Slow down traffic on interconnected streets by using traffic calming measures. Plan for regional commercial facilities in regional centers. In smaller communities, plan for commercial facilities by inventorying infill opportunities and adopting regulations that limit building scale and establish site design requirements. Change zoning standards for commercial and industrial buildings to fit structures on smaller lots, to build up to the street, and to share parking with neighbors.

If you work as a *planner* or *land conservation* or *economic development specialist*, you have the opportunity to help implement compact development and land preservation. Work with nonprofit affordable housing groups and use state funds to rehabilitate vacant and underused village buildings, creating retail and offices on the ground floor and apartments upstairs.

Identify infill opportunities in urban and village centers and work with the private sector and nonprofit organizations to develop these sites. Identify good examples of mixed-use and mixed-income development to illustrate opportunities. Enlist major employers to participate in planning for new, mixed-use town centers. Keep the land productive and encourage passage of farms to future generations by using state and private funds to buy development rights. Protect high elevation environments for wildlife habitat, water quality, outdoor recreation, and wild and scenic character by fundraising or issuing a town bond.

If yours is a *nonprofit organization*, you may have an important role in the future of your community. Affordable housing groups can reach out to people in need by finding them safe and sanitary housing while rehabilitating deteriorated neighborhoods. Conservation commissions, environmental groups, and land trusts can encourage development that protects natural resources while contributing to healthy neighborhoods and town centers. Instead of, or in addition to, opposing bad development, you can support good development. Historic preservation organizations can work to make town centers attractive for businesses that will, in turn, help to restore buildings.

If you are a *legislator* or a *public official* involved in setting policy, you can play a role in changing the direction of contemporary development. Support legislation that implements policies and programs that support compact growth centers. Work on state legislation to require municipalities to permit accessory housing units with single-family homes. Give alternative transportation or the repair of existing roads and bridges priority over the construction of new highways. Reexamine local, state, and federal public investment policies and practices, making changes to keep facilities such as town offices, libraries, schools, court houses, and post offices in town centers.

If you are a *developer*, your impact is great. Build for the future, taking a long-term view of your investment. Build in a compact, pedestrian-oriented pattern, on land within an existing settlement. Redevelop brownfields and other underused sites, adding density where infrastructure already exists. Understand the market for traditional neighborhoods in your area. Build small lot housing with big lot amenities. Mix housing types within neighborhoods while limiting heights and scale to fit in with overall neighborhood character. Provide public "social" spaces, such as town greens, streets, schools, town halls, restaurants, and stores. Make sure that the scale and use of your projects fit the needs and character of the area.

Businesses are part of the solution as well. One size doesn't fit all in rural communities. Don't assume that your development formula is going to work everywhere. Make the most of the space you have before you consider building on a greenfield site. Explore locations where people can walk or bicycle or use transit to reach you. Put your parking out back and focus your entry on the street. The way that business treads on the land, how your employees get to work, and what type of housing your employees live in are important to your bottom line—and that of the community.

We hope the examples throughout this book will inspire the many players who shape the land to act now. We encourage you to take a close look at your communities from the air and from the ground, through your regulations and plans, and with an eye toward the trends that are affecting the landscape and community vitality. Try on some of these ideas and see how they fit. Contact other communities to see how they are addressing these issues. Look from above and see beyond.

Brattleboro Area Community Land Trust
5.24

Burlington Department of Public Works
8.15

Julie Campoli
2.1, 2.5-2.14, 2.22,.2.24-2.28, 2.34-2.36, 3.9, 3.10, 3.12, 3.18, 3.23, 3.29, 3.35, 3.36, 4.6-4.10, 4.12-4.15, 5.6-5.9, 5.13, 5.19, 5.23, 6.13-6.15, 6.20, 6.22, 6.24-6.27, 7.2, 7.8, 7.9, 8.4, 8.5-8.7, 8.10, 8.13, 8.14, 8.16, 8.17-8.19, 8.23, 8.25-8.30

Dan Higgins
3.30

Elizabeth Humstone
3.4, 3.8, 3.14-3.16, 3.25, 5.14, 5.20-5.22, 5.25, 7.6, 7.7

Alex MacLean
I.1, 1.1-1.14, 2.2, 2.4, 2.15, 2.19, 2.23, 2.29, 2.33, 3.1-3.3, 3.6, 3.7, 3.13, 3.17, 3.21, 3.24, 3.26-3.28, 3.31, 4.1, 4.3, 4.5, 4.16, 4.18, 4.26, 5.1, 5.3-5.5, 5.10, 5.12, 5.15-5.18, 6.1, 6.2, 6.9-6.12, 6.16, 6.21, 6.23, 7.1, 7.3, 7.5, 7.10-7.12, 7.14-7.21, 7.23-7.25, 8.1, 8.8, 8.9, 8.11, 8.12, 8.31, 8.32

MacLean/Campoli
I.2, 2.3, 2.16-2.18, 2.20, 2.21, 2.30-2.32, 3.5, 3.11, 3.20, 3.33, 3.34, 3.37, 3.38, 4.2, 4.4, 4.11, 4.19-4.24, 4.26, 4.27, 5.2, 5.11, 6.17-6.19, 7.4, 7.13, 7.22, 8.2, 8.3, 8.20, 8.21, 8.22, 8.24

Maine State Planning Office
4.17

Truex, Cullins, and Partners
3.32

University of Vermont Remote Sensing Lab
3.19

Vermont Historical Society
3.22, 6.3 - 6.8

Arendt, Randall. *Crossroads, Hamlet, Village, Town: Design Characteristics of Traditional Neighborhoods, Old and New*, Planning Advisory Service Report Number 487/488, Chicago, American Planning Association, 1999.

Berger, K.T. *Where the Sky and the Road Collide: America Through the Eyes of its Drivers*, New York, Henry Holt, 1993.

Blakely, Edward J., and Mary G. Snyder. *Fortress America: Gated Communities in the United States*, Washington, D.C., Brookings Institution, and Cambridge, Massachusetts, Lincoln Institute of Land Policy, 1997.

Bloomer, Kent, and Charles Moore. *Body, Memory and Architecture*, New Haven and London, Yale University Press, 1977.

Calthorpe, Peter. *The Next American Metropolis: Ecology, Community, and the New American Dream*, New York, Princeton Architectural Press, 1993.

Champlain Initiative. *The History of Sprawl in Chittenden County*, Burlington, Vermont, March 1999.

Clay, Grady. *Close-Up: How to Read the American City*, New York, Praeger Publishers, 1973.

Cronon, William, et al. *Uncommon Ground: Toward Reinventing Nature*, New York, W.W. Norton, 1995.

Daniels, Tom. *When City and Country Collide: Managing Growth on the Metropolitan Fringe*, Washington, D.C., Island Press, 1999.

Drew, Bettina. *Crossing the Expendable Landscape*, St. Paul, Grey Wolf Press, 1998.

Duany, Andres, Elizabeth Plater-Zyberk, and Jeff Speck. *Suburban Nation: The Rise of Sprawl and the Decline of the American Dream*, New York, North Point Press, 2000.

Dulken, Diane. "Foot Traffic," *Planning*, June 1999, pp. 16-17.

Eagan, Timothy. *Lasso the Wind: Away to the New West*, New York, Knopf, 1998.

Ellin, Nan, ed. *Architecture of Fear*, New York, Princeton Architectural Press, 1997.

Ewing, Reid, and Robert Hodder. *Best Development Practices, A Primer for Smart Growth*, Smart Growth Network, no date.

Federal Housing Administration. "Successful Subdivisions," *Land Planning Bulletin No. 1*, U.S. Government Printing Office, Washington, D.C., 1940.

Fleming, Ronald Lee. *Saving Face: How Corporate Franchise Design Can Respect Community Identity*, Planning Advisory Service Report No. 452, Chicago, American Planning Association, 1994.

Gallagher, Winifred. *The Power of Place: How Our Surroundings Shape Our Thoughts, Emotions, and Actions*, New York, Harper Collins, 1994.

Groth, Paul and Todd W. Bressi, et al. *Understanding Ordinary Landscapes*, New Haven, Yale University Press, 1997.

Hale, Jonathan. *The Old Way of Seeing: How Architecture Lost Its Magic and How to Get it Back*, Boston, Houghton Mifflin, 1994.

Harris, Steven, and Deborah Berke. *Architecture of the Everyday*, New York, Princeton Architectural Press, 1997.

Hayden, Dolores. *The Power of Place: Urban Landscapes as Public History*, Cambridge, Massachusetts, MIT Press, 1997.

HCPC, Inc. and Planimetrics, LLP. *The Costs of Suburban Sprawl and Urban Decay in Rhode Island*, Grow Smart Rhode Island, Providence, Rhode Island, December, 1999.

Hough, Michael. *Out of Place: Restoring Identity to the Regional Landscape*, New Haven, Yale University Press, 1990.

Hunter, Malcolm L. *Wildlife, Forests, and Forestry: Principles for Managing Forests for Biological Diversity*, Englewood Cliffs, New Jersey, Prentice Hall, 1990.

Hylton, Thomas. *Save Our Land, Save Our Towns*, Harrisburg, Pennsylvania, RB Books, 1995.

Jacobs, Jane. *The Death and Life of Great American Cities*, New York, Random House, 1961.

Kay, Jane Holtz. *Asphalt Nation. How the Automobile Took Over America and How We Can Take it Back*, New York, Crown Publishers, 1997.

Kelbaugh, Douglas. *Common Place: Toward Neighborhood and Regional Design*, Seattle, University of Washington Press, 1997.

Kemis, Daniel. *Community and the Politics of Place*, Norman, University of Oklahoma Press, 1990.

Klyza, Christopher McGrory, and Stephen C Trombulak. *The Story of Vermont: A Natural and Cultural History*, Hanover, New Hampshire, University Press of New England, 1999.

Knack, Ruth Eckdish. "Cutting Monster Houses Down to Size," *Planning*, October 1999, pp. 4-9.

Kunstler, James Howard. *Home From Nowhere: Remaking Our Everyday World for the 21st Century*, New York, Touchstone, 1998.

Leach, William. *Country of Exiles*, New York, Pantheon, 1999.

Lofland, Lyn H. *The Public Realm*, New York, Aldine De Gruyter, 1998.

Maine State Planning Office, *Markets for Traditional Neighborhoods*, Augusta, Maine, August 1999.

Martin, Judith A., and Sam Bass Warner. "Urban Conservation: Sociable, Green and Affordable," *Placing Nature*, Washington, D.C., Island Press, 1997.

McKenzie, Evan. *Privatopia: Homeowner Associations and the Rise of Residential Private Government*, New Haven, Yale University Press, 1994.

Moe, Richard, and Carter Wilkie. *Changing Places: Rebuilding Communities in the Age of Sprawl*, New York, Henry Holt, 1997.

Mogelonsky, Marcia. "Reconfiguring the American Dream," *American Demograhics*, January 1997.

National Association of Local Government Environmental Professionals. *Profiles of Business Leadership on Smart Growth*, Washington, D.C., 1999.

Nelessen, Anton. *Visions for a New American Dream: Process, Principles and an Ordinance to Plan and Design Small Communities*, Chicago, American Planning Association, 1994.

New Jersey Office of State Planning. Regional Centers and the Future of Large Scale Employment Facilities, *Nine Critical Development Issues*, January 1999.

Oldenburg, Ray. *The Great Good Place*, New York, Marlowe and Company, 1989.

Perin, Constance. *Everything in its Place: Social Order and Land Use in America*, Princeton, New Jersey, Princeton University Press, 1977.

Price, Jennifer. *Flight Maps*, New York, Basic Books, 1999.

PricewaterhouseCoopers LLP and Lend Lease Real Estate Investments, Inc. *Emerging Trends in Real Estate*, New York, October 1999.

Putnam, Robert B. *Bowling Alone: The Collapse and Revival of American Community*, New York, Simon and Schuster, 2000.

Reps, John. *The Making of Urban America*, Princeton, New Jersey, Princeton University Press, 1965.

Ryden, Kent. *Mapping the Invisible Landscape*, Iowa City, University of Iowa Press, 1993.

Schmitt, Peter J. *Back to Nature: The Arcadian Myth in Urban America*, New York, Oxford University Press, 1969.

Soloman, Daniel. *Rebuilding*. New York, Princeton Architectural Press, 1992.

Sorkin, Michael, et al. *Variations on a Theme Park: The New American City and the End of Public Space*, New York, Hill and Wang, 1992.

Southworth, Michael, and Eran Ben-Joseph. *Streets and the Shaping of Towns and Cities*, New York, McGraw Hill, 1997.

Stein, Clarence. *Toward New Towns for America*, New York, 1957.

Stilgoe, John R. Borderlands. *Origins of the American Suburb 1820-1939*, New Haven, Yale University Press, 1988.

Surface Transportation Policy Project. *High Mileage Moms*, January 13, 2000.

Teyssot, Georges. *The American Lawn*, New York, Princeton Architectural Press, 1999.

University of Vermont Historic Preservation Students. *Finding Space Downtown*, for Vermont Forum on Sprawl, Burlington, Vermont, April 2000.

Vermont Forum on Sprawl. *Exploring Sprawl #1, Vermonters' Attitudes on Sprawl*, Burlington, Vermont, February 1999.

Vermont Forum on Sprawl. *Exploring Sprawl #5, The Costs of Development: Downtowns vs. Open Space*, Burlington, Vermont, 1999.

Vermont Forum on Sprawl. *Exploring Sprawl #6, Economic, Social, and Land Use Trends Related to Sprawl in Vermont*, Burlington, Vermont, 1999.

Vermont Division for Historic Preservation. Vermont Historic Preservation Plan, Transportation Theme, Montpelier, Vermont, July 1989.

Wessels, Tom. *Reading the Forested Landscape: A Natural History of New England*. Woodstock, The Countryman Press, 1997.

Yacos, Karen. *A Study of Sprawl in Eight Vermont Communities*, Vermont Forum on Sprawl, Burlington, Vermont, December 1998.